Life-Belief

A Faith for All

(Revised and Augmented)

Alistair J. Sinclair Ph.D.

AP
Almostic

Almostic Publications

Published by

Almostic Publications

London

ISBN 978-1-7396937-0-1

© 2022, 2025 Alistair J. Sinclair

Other Works by Alistair J. Sinclair

BOOKS
The Answers Lie Within Us
What is Philosophy: An Introduction
The Will to Live: A Systematic Guide to Our Reasons for Living
American Papers in Humanism and Religion
The Promise of Dualism: An Introduction to Dualist Theory
Hale and Hearty: Looking at Things as a Whole
Advancing Humanity: The Need to Make Our Own Future
Belief Beyond Belief: Looking to a Better Future
The Way of Togetherness: Hope for the Future in a Godless World
Jesus of Nazareth: The Real Man and his Message
Sagacity: The Way to Wisdom
Words of Support: Life is not Meaningless or Pointless
The Ubiquity of Reciprocity: An Introduction to Reciprocal Philosophy
All About Time: Time for Itself, the Universe and Shakespeare

E-BOOKS
The Future of Humanity: The Need to Believe in Humanity and its Future
From Time to Eternity: An Essay on the Meaning of Time
Shakespeare on Time
Punish the Person not the Crime: A New Theory of Punishment Based on
Old Principles
Old Age, Death and the After-Life
Reforming the British Constitution
The Middle Way versus Extremism

ONLINE PAPERS
The Making of the Scottish Enlightenment: The Role of Self-improvement
in Scottish Clubs and Societies
The Failure of Thomas Reid's attack on David Hume
World War One and the Loss of the Humanist Consensus
What to do About Religion: A Plan of Action
A Humanist's Faith: Towards a Humanist Alternative to Religion
Henry Ford: The Visionary Humanist
Dualism and Humanism
The Need for the Dualist View to Combat Extremism
Inverted Universe Theory: Fact or Fiction?
Imperialism versus Nationalism: A World Without War (WWW)

Contents

Part Five – Bringing Religions Together

Part Six –The Practical Application in the Community

The diagram on the front cover of this book contains the Saltire flag of Scotland and the Ankh in the centre which represents life. The two stars are of Sinclair tartans – the ancient and the hunting tartans. The heraldic emblems are of the city of Dunfermline on the left and the city of Dundee on the right. I was born in the former city and educated in the latter.

Preface

This book is the culmination of much thought and writing on reconciling religion with my humanist beliefs. In papers such as "A Humanist's Faith: Towards a Humanist Alternative to Religion", I developed many of the views expressed in this book. Secular humanists have usually been dismissive of, if not downright hostile towards, religion. But religious minded humanists have always sought to find a place for religion. This book takes these humanistic views and transcends them to put human beings into the context of life itself of which we are only one specimen and a flawed one at that. Life-belief puts human beings in their place without making more of them than they deserve, which is not a lot at this time.

Nevertheless, there is nothing to beat the marvellous gift of life, and it surely deserves to be celebrated for its own sake, regardless of religious considerations. Celebrating life is what this book is about while, at the same time, taking account of religions and their diverse sentiments.

There is no room for religious resignation or monkish silence in life-belief. It is about living life to the full. This is *vivoplenia* involving the principle of plenitude. It means speaking out when things go wrong with the world and not remaining silent, as expressed in this poem by my poetical school friend, Ian Speed:

Qui tacet consentire videtur
(He who is silent appears to consent)

Take a break from your screen
put it on pause if you'd like:
think what's truly of value,
what you'd always speak up for:
I don't hear you-
are you listening to me?

Take a break from your break,
catch your breath, clear your head:
think what you'd fight for,
defend with your life, body on line:
anything come to mind?
is your conscience awake?

Find a darkened room,
sit quietly, make self invisible to all:
reflect on how you are duped,
dumbed down, controlled:

Now, use your voice-
he who is silent appears to consent.

Introduction

In this book, the notion of life-belief is used as way of reconciling religion with science and the modern world. It emphasises the need to believe in life more than in any other belief. This view does not threaten religion but only attacks the most extreme applications of religion. It is religious extremism which is objectionable and not religion as such. The various religions must take their respective places in society and be tolerant of other beliefs and faiths. Religious people need to understand what atheists and humanists are saying and respect their right to hold such beliefs. Above all, they must acknowledge the benefits of science to humanity.

Life-belief is therefore about believing in what science is telling us about life. Realistically, it means assuming: (1) that purpose only exists in the universe because of the purposefulness of life forms, (2) that life emerged on Earth through natural processes, and (3) that we come out of nothing at birth and return to nothing at death. What lies between birth and death is our 'life' which we free to make as much or as little of as we can or wish. Part Two (see pp. 8-14) deals with such presuppositions in more detail. The importance of life-belief for religion is promoted here. It provides a focal point that disciplines all religions (and, indeed, ideologies) in relation to the needs of life and humanity. In that way, humanity can move forward in unison instead of being torn apart by dissension and disharmony, not to mention war, conflict and hatred.

A distinct religion is not intended here, as there are already enough religions around. It is a way to bring religions together for the benefit of humanity as a whole. It is about broadening minds with an additional way of looking at religion and its role in society. We can all believe in life but religions in the past have not always put much value on human life. Thus, life-belief is about valuing everyone's life regardless of their religious persuasions, which is basically the humanist position (see pp. 32-3 below).

Life-belief does not mean making more of life than it really is. Life is not being divinised or given a spiritual or platonic existence. Belief in life is personal to each of us. It is an extreme view to abstract the idea of life from our personal affairs as is done, for example, by anti-abortionists (see page 6 for more on that). Believing in life is about the living of it and not the deification of it. A philosophy of *living* is intended by this book.

Life-belief means believing that our lives are valuable and worth living. It is a faith that everyone can believe in if they need one. It is the fall-back faith that remains even when all other faiths fall by the wayside. Even if we hardly give it a thought, it is common to us all unless we are obsessed with death or in a death cult of some sort. Anyone who puts death before life is hardly living at all. Even those without any beliefs may still believe in the importance of life. They may believe that their own lives are not important but still believe that life itself is important.

Life-belief or *Vivodoxia* (to give it a fancy name) consists in believing in the value of life itself. *'Vivodoxia'* means 'life believing', and it is surely something we may all agree with. We can all be Vivodoxians believing in life above all else. It is more about living life than just life in the abstract.

Life-belief is the most basic faith of all. We can believe what we like, and it is not necessary for a Vivodoxian to believe in God, Jesus, Moses, Mohammed, the Buddha or any of the many entities, prophets or belief systems inflicted on humanity over the ages in religion's name. All our beliefs can be boiled down to a simple belief in life for its own sake and for nothing else. But religions are not being jettisoned in favour of life-belief as it is a faith not incompatible with other faiths, as is argued below.

The belief in the value of life may be implicit in all religions but it is not made totally explicit. It is not brought to the fore in any clear and unequivocal way. As a result, the fanatics of practically every religion have had no qualms about taking life in the name of their religion. They are liable to kill people with whom they do not agree. Unless life-belief is made an important part of every religion, as it ought to be, the extremists will find excuses to disregard the value of human life in order to impose their views on people. This faith of life-belief aims to remedy that defect and make the protection and nurturing of life paramount. The aim is to ensure that the taking of life in the name of religion becomes anathema as a consequence of life-belief being universally adopted.

My life is sacred just as the lives of everyone, indeed, of all living beings are sacred and irreplaceable. What is sacred about this philosophy is life, living and the processes of the universe that have made life possible. This is a down-to-earth and material view. The sanctity of life is material in that it refers to the actuality of life and living. It is not merely spiritual but a matter of how we live our lives for the better.

If life-belief is universally accepted, it could bring together all religions in sharing the common faith of believing in life. Religious people can be more content with their differences from each other within the broad framework of life-belief. The religions would be less inclined to compete and vie with each other for people's attention. As the importance of life is obvious to everyone, the hope is that all religions will concentrate more on what they have in common and less on their differences. The aim is therefore to cultivate the spirit of harmony and unity among humanity.

Life-belief is not a fixed body of doctrine; it is a dynamic, dualistic and interactionist belief that helps people to make the most of their lives. This dynamic orientation towards people saves it from the extremism, dogmatism and narrowness to which religions are often prone. Workability is than any adherence to preconceived doctrines.

As life is sacred and common to us, this faith in life transcends all religious faiths. All religions are subsumed under a higher faith. The hope is that humanity can then move forward in unison instead of being divided by antagonistic faiths.

There are therefore two approaches in this elucidation of life-belief (1) the togetherness theme and (2) the right-thinking theme. Togetherness sets the stage for bringing religions together, and right-thinking or righteousness is about making the most of life and living. These two strands are intertwined in the arguments throughout this book.

This book gives the basic presuppositions for this life-belief, and it proclaims the fullness of life as an aim that we can also have in common. Atheism also is compatible with this view. The inclusivity of life-belief is therefore made clear and it is potentially beneficial to all.

Presuppositions. This life-belief view is elucidated here in a rational way that is also compatible with the scientific view of the universe. It provides an interface between science and religion. Life-belief means believing in the findings of science at least as much as in the exhortations of Holy Scripture. As the presuppositions of life-belief are based on the findings of science, the acceptance of life-belief will hopefully make religious thinking more accommodating to these findings. This is the role of the presuppositions outlined in Part Two below, pages 8 to 14.

Plenitude. Believing in a full life is as important as believing in life itself. An empty life is not worth living. A full life is one that is purposeful and self-fulfilling. The drug of living life to the full surpasses all other drugs or artificial stimulants. This view is supported and elaborated in the Principle of Plenitude which is the subject of Part Three, pages 16 to 28.

Strengthening. Life-belief is strengthened by the humanist, holist, universalist, prospectivist and unifying views. These show that there is more to believing in life alone. This is because of the complexity of life itself. That complexity makes life more self-sufficient, self-preservative, and reproductive in one way or another. This is discussed in Part Four, pages 30 to 54.

Inclusivity. Potentially, life-belief includes all the religions that value life for its own sake. It also means finding interest and value in all religions. If we make the effort to explore and understand all the different religions then a coming together of diverse religious communities becomes a real possibility. This is argued in Part Five, pages 56 to 63.

Anti-Exclusionarianism. If life-belief is indeed universally accepted then it helps religions to become more inclusive and less exclusive. They can take their place in the community as community centres that are no longer exclusive to themselves or counter-community. The community aspects of life-belief are discussed in Part Six below, pages 65 to 69.

Part One

The Basics

The Importance of Believing in Life

A belief in life overrides all other religious beliefs; a lifeless religion is inconceivable. A belief system that does not believe in life is not a religion but some kind of malign cult, perhaps satanic, nihilistic or necrophiliac in nature. Life-belief or Vivodoxia therefore provides a focal point for all religions within which they can function at an individual level. Every religious person can practise their religion while freely adopting Vivodoxia as a belief system that they hold in common with every other religious person. It need not contradict or stand in the way of their religious faith. Belief in life encourages us to bring our own meaning into existence without which the universe is meaningless in every respect. By such meaning we ensure that our future differs favourably from our past.

There is no question of worshipping life or making a god out of life. We only acknowledge its true importance in the physical universe. We do not elevate life in a spiritual way out of its material existence. It is what it is and it need not be considered divine or spiritual. It is the spontaneous product of the physical forces of the universe, and it needs no justification other than itself. Life arose through an ever-increasing internal complexity brought about by purposeful activity (the process of *complexification*). Life did this all by itself without divine intervention. (See page 52 for more on this.)

Life is the crowning glory of the Earth. Some may disagree. They see life as a festering slime on the surface of the planet. But this is a narrow, negative viewpoint. Within the context of the universe as a whole, we can see life's importance. It is the culmination of an inner complexity that gives our planet the majesty and enthronement that few planets possess.

The idea of life is unique to intelligent beings. Human beings are like other life-forms in struggling for life and in enjoying it when we can. However, we are not like other life-forms on this planet in that we can think of life as an abstract notion whereas they live their lives without knowing what life is. We know not only what life is but also how important it is. Only intelligent beings like us can know that life is at the apogee of entity existence in the universe.

Life-forms are more complexified than non-organic entities. Their internalised complexity makes them purposeful entities that make goals and aims within themselves as they strive to survive by eating and defending themselves. As a result, life has more to offer the universe in terms of purposefulness than other less complexified entities. It brings purpose into existence that can't exist otherwise. That alone makes life worth fighting for to ensure that it is sustained and that its propagation throughout the universe is maintained. Thus, our primary, self-appointed purpose must be to support that propagation of life. Admittedly, that process has scarcely begun as our ability to exploit outer space is still in its infancy, despite the promise of the 1960s and 70s lunar landings.

Life is a part of nature but by no means subordinate to it. Nature is both the friend and foe of life. It nurtures as much as it annihilates. It is not just 'red in tooth and claw'[1]; it also provides sustenance and great beauty and inspiration, as it includes vegetation, flowers, clouds, scenery, and sunny days; but also tornadoes, earthquakes and tsunamis. Life is successful when it works with nature and is neither entirely predominant over it nor abjectly submissive to it. We need to relate realistically to nature and get into balance with the planet and everything in it.

However, this rebalancing with nature is not achievable by going back to a more primitive 'state of nature'. Primitive tribes were even more destructive of nature as they changed the flora and fauna radically by wiping out whole species and changing the vegetation and the landscape in which they lived. Not only the mammoth but also many interesting species of South America, New Zealand and elsewhere did not survive the coming of man. The earliest inhabitants of Australia changed the landscape by their use of fire. To get more in touch with nature we need to organise ourselves more straightforwardly and reduce our dependence on the planet. This means economic and technological progress and not the reverse. By being more organised and economical in our use of materials, we can make progress by simplifying our lives and becoming more efficient in our use of resources. There is more on this in my book *Advancing Humanity: The Need to Make our own Future,* (Almostic Publications, 2016).

Life-Belief Makes Meaning

Believing in life implies that life has some meaning. Life in the abstract has meaning because it refers to the most complex forms of entity in the universe i.e. life-forms. Life's unique position in the universe makes it admirable and worth revering. But our own lives as individuals are even more important to us. These lives stand in most need of belief and meaningfulness. For life *means* what we think it is, and the act of giving meaning to our lives is precisely what we are living to do.

If we accept the view that we make our own meaning in life, then the meaning of life is the meaning we put into it, get out of it, make of it or find in it. What we do with our lives confers meaning on them. Our lives have no meaning at all in isolation from what we make of them. We might choose to regard everything we do as meaningless and fruitless but that is only a choice and is not the whole truth of the matter. We may choose to think of our lives as being meaningless when we are in the mood to do so. But that does not make them so.

Seeing everything as meaningless is a matter of emotional mood; it is an attitude that changes just as all our moods do. A suicidal frame of mind similarly depends on a person being in the mood for it, and when the mood fades so does the need to do it, even if only temporarily. Many people who survive suicide attempts go on to live satisfying lives. To avoid such states of mind, we must continually make the effort to find and create meaning and expel negative feelings. The truth always includes the other side of the coin, or indeed is the silver lining to the dark cloud.

As life forms, we are the creators of meaning in the universe. It can never be repeated too often that there is no meaning in the universe except what is brought into existence by living beings pursuing their ingiven purposes. They require no external agents to provide meaning or to give them the power to find meaning. They arrive at meanings *firstly* to preserve and prolong their existence as identifiable and distinguishable entities and *secondly* to nourish and enrich their lives. Their inner complexity is such that they require meaningfulness to preserve their being and make sense of their lives. Otherwise their unity and integrity would only be short lived and they would be unable to pass on their inner complexity through reproduction or cultural dissemination. It is the complexity of the inner interactions that makes living beings distinct from mere material objects that lack a life of their own. (See page 52 for more on the role of complexity in bringing life into being.)

Meaning means doing. In common with all living beings, human beings find meaning by doing things and this makes us doers or agents. Doing involves interacting. We connect with things and make them meaningful to ourselves by that connection. If I touch a table with a fingertip, I am interacting with it by means of nerve impulses that are activated by contact with table's surface, and these impulses travel back and forth between the fingertip and my brain. The impulses convey and confirm the feeling which the act of touching gives me. The feeling has meaning for me because I have interacted with something distinct from myself. I identify with the object because of that feeling which is mine alone. Interacting thus involves meaning when the agent finds it in the act of feeling, seeing, speaking, writing, or whatever. Thus, the ultimate meaning of life for each of us lies in doing things which are meaningful to us. In everything that we do for a reason, we are creating meaning that did not previously exist.

In creating meaning we become responsible for the future of all life, since everything that we do has ramifications that stretch near and far, and perhaps in ways beyond our present comprehension, as quantum physics seems to tell us. The meaning created by intelligent beings is also important in that it is self-reflective and self-critical. By self-examination, we can ascertain the value of what we are doing and the good and bad effects of our deeds. This implies that intelligent beings such as ourselves are potentially the most accountable of all entities in the universe.

Our self-awareness makes us responsible for our surroundings. Seeing the plight of our planet makes us want to do something about it. We become responsible for life because we know what life means for the future of the universe. Without the burgeoning of life in the universe, it has no meaning. As the future of life is always precarious, we can give meaning to our lives by dedicating ourselves to the cultivation and propagation of life. We then become responsible for the plight of life in the universe and can justify our existence by doing everything we can to nurture life and further it. That responsibility cannot be shirked without denying our self-knowledge of what we are and underestimating what we can do as a species, as many pro-religionists and anti-humanists are prone to do in undermining our status in this universe.

How life finds meaning in the universe. The vastness of the universe is an opportunity for life and humanity and not a drawback. Science teaches us that we live in a huge and mainly material universe that is subject to unique physical laws and arbitrary chance events. From that point of view, the universe means nothing at all apart from the chance and necessity of events that govern it. We and other living beings are only tiny, tenuous vestiges of self-awareness in an otherwise vast and indifferent material universe. But these are not dismal facts when we consider that the vast amounts of matter and energy are an endless resource for living beings to tap into. In a manner of speaking, we are seeded into this vast universe and have only begun to grow. This fact encourages us to use this resource to our own ends since there is apparently nothing in the universe to prevent us doing so except our own inertia and lack of self-belief. We can therefore accept our material insignificance with cheerful equanimity considering how meaningful and joyful we can make our lives despite such material considerations. The right attitude of mind is needed and instilling it is a task for Vivodoxians.

The Open and Friendly Faith

Life-belief is a friendly faith that favours openness, honesty, straightforwardness. It aims studiously to avoid nastiness and hatred as being counterproductive. It is a wide-open faith that excludes no one, whatever their beliefs or the lack of them. Life-belief holds the position midway between outright scepticism and dogmatic belief. This is the open-minded view characteristic of the scientific view at its best – when it avoids dogmatic scientism that proclaims the supremacy of science, or takes it to unacceptable extremes by making science inhuman or over-objective.

Science cannot give us all the answers and it does not claim to do so. It is indispensable to our lives but only within strict limits, as its findings are easily taken to extremes. Scientists make mistakes and may defend their findings against all evidence to the contrary. The imperfections of science make it a human enterprise but where its theories are shown to work and the evidence supports them, it can be relied upon.

Religion is also taken to extremes when its absurdities and mysteries are enforced without limit preventing critical thinking. Whoever believes uncritically in such matters is liable to believe anything whatsoever and be the dupe of charlatans, bigots and conspiracy theorists. Life-belief can moderate all these extremes by putting all faiths in their proper perspective as personal beliefs instead of absolute truths.

Moderation goes hand in hand with wisdom. An informed wisdom is ever open to continuous development in the light of further thought, experience and information. It gives substance to the practical kind of wisdom characteristic of wise men down the ages. We keep to the path of truth in being open-minded and by freely inquiring into things. An open mind pursues truth by pouring light on things and moving forward to greater enlightenment, whereas a closed mind remains stuck in the false darkness of self-centredness. The path of truth is fringed on both sides by error and ignorance that lead us into darkness and depression. There is more about the importance of wisdom below in Part Three on Plenitude pages 16 to 28, and in my book *Sagacity: The Way to Wisdom* (Almostic Publications, 2019).

The Prominence of Religion

Religion is a prominent part of our society, but it tends to be excessively exclusive. The various religions hive themselves off from each other, and this prevents them from belonging to society wholeheartedly. This applies particularly to extreme cults and sects that cut themselves off altogether. It can lead to the collective suicide of the sect. We are all the worse for this exclusivity as it increases the differences between people and is a constant source of conflict and enmity. This book is about making religion more inclusive and participative in society. This is important for the togetherness of society and of the whole world, as argued in my book, *The Way of Togetherness,* (Almostic Publications, 2018)

The religions of the world are apt to compete with each other for the world's attention, and they become antagonistic towards each other. Something more is needed to bring them together in the interests of common humanity. The various religions cannot be serving humanity when they pit themselves against the rest of humanity and disparage those not of their faith. Life-belief can be the common faith with which all other faiths agree. It may serve as a religion of all religions that tops them all without threatening any of them. Perhaps it can then bring people together in a framework common to all of us.

It is possible for the various religions to be good and positive when they are life-enhancing. Life is believed in irrespective of other beliefs or the lack of them. It is not even necessary to believe in life-belief as such. It is sufficient only to understand it, since understanding it implies that the person is participating in life by living through what life means to them. No one can think or act without proving the fact that they are living and are therefore a part of what life is, just as animals and plants are.

This is not to believe in life fanatically or obsessively. There are limits to that belief, just as there are limits to all beliefs. Life cannot be supported beyond all reason. When our lives begin and when they end, are not necessarily in our control. We are liable to live and die arbitrarily, even with the best medical expertise. In order to live, we must ourselves kill living beings. Vegetarians kill plant life to live, and even if they live on fruit alone, this deprives seeds of the opportunity to live. As mentioned above, nature itself is prolific in its destruction of life – it is "red in tooth and claw". Most human pregnancies miscarry, often without the mother knowing about it, so that miscarriage is "the predominant outcome of fertilisation" and "a natural and inevitable part of human reproduction at all ages."[2] Human abortion is no more anti-life than natural miscarriage; it differs only in giving the mother a choice in the matter. While the foetus remains an intimate part of her body, without which it cannot live, she is entitled to that choice. Her life may depend on it, whereas the potential viability of the foetus cannot be relied upon with absolute certainty.

Bringing all religions together. It is possible that all religions can be brought together through a deeper understanding of what they are and how they contribute to life and humanity. Life-belief offers a common framework of thought that can moderate their excesses and reduce the extremism to which they are prone. It promotes the study and appreciation of all religions without favouring any particular religion. Vivodoxia brings religions together by studying them and showing what they have in common. It is not to be imposed on people as if it were the religion to end all other religions. It is the religion within which all other religions can be studied and appreciated.

Religions on their own are isolated and exclusive organisations which behave as if they have all the answers that must be accepted without question by anyone belonging to that religion. Jonathan Swift wrote "We have just enough religion to make us hate, but not enough to make us love one another."[3] A religion that incorporates all religions could be enough religion to make us all love one another. Within the aegis of Vivodoxia every religion can take its place without sacrificing its belief content.

Part Two

The Presuppositions

The Role of Presuppositions

The presuppositions of life-belief reflect what immediately springs to mind in holding this belief. They clarify what it means to believe in life and its value. Moreover, they are assumptions influenced by current scientific knowledge. They presuppose a degree of understanding of science and its limitations. For that reason, the list of presuppositions given here is not complete or definitive. They can be deleted, augmented, altered, revised and improved as our view of life and the universe changes and improves. For instance, we might even discard the eighth presupposition on the inevitability of death if we can find a way of prolonging our lives indefinitely.

It is important at least to understand these presuppositions though there is no need to agree entirely with them. They are not meant to be enforced as gospel truths. They are food for thought and not a catechism to be learnt by rote. Though it is enough simply to believe in life, full stop, the presuppositions are a guide to what can be believed about life, when we go beyond the simplest appreciation of life. Anyone who does not believe at all in life may need help, whether sympathetic, psychiatric or whatever. Those who want their lives to end for therapeutic or other reasons may still believe in the value of life. Some important presuppositions of life-belief are outlined as follows:

First Presupposition of Life-Belief

The Importance of Life: When the universe came into existence, it became something in place of nothing. When life came into existence, it became possible for the universe to be known to be something rather than nothing.

Corollary: It is a perennial question among philosophers why there is something rather than nothing. The probability is that there should be nothing at all. The universe has apparently defied mega-astronomical odds to come into being and with the physical laws and forces necessary for life to emerge, at least on planet Earth. Life, in the form of intelligent beings like ourselves, ensures that the universe is known to exist by way of self-reference. The universe provided the physical conditions that enabled us to come into being. In being a part of the universe, we are now the means by which the universe refers back on itself to have knowledge of its contents, its history and its outcome. Life is therefore an important development for the universe in that respect. Without life, the universe does indeed make no sense at all. In believing in life, we can appreciate its importance in coming into being at all when the odds are that nothing should exist. We can therefore believe in life simply because it is unique in having come into being at all.

8

Second Presupposition of Life-Belief

The Complexification of Life: Life is not only the product of the physical forces of the universe; it also progresses and proliferates by complexification and not just by replication.

Corollary: Life is the gift of the universe, not as creator but as facilitator. The universe has made life possible, not by creating it according to any plan but by means of the complexifying processes made possible by physical forces bringing things together. These processes have produced ever more complex elements culminating in the complex life forms of which we human beings are an important part. There is no set plan as to how different life forms came into being any more than there is a set plan as to how a tree branches out as it grows, or how the whorls on our finger tips are created.

Life forms are material bodies that are more internally developed and involved than non-organic material bodies. They are subject to a complexification process of ever-increasing internal complexity which accumulates over time. The accumulated complexity is passed on through successive life-forms and has culminated in complex behaviour of human beings. Human society is, as far as we know, the more complex entity known to us in the universe. But even without us, life can achieve amazing things by continuing its complexification beyond the current achievements of human beings.

Third Presupposition of Life-Belief

The Importance of Meaning: A belief in life encourages us to bring our own meaning into existence without which the universe is meaningless in every respect. By such meaning we ensure that our future differs from our past.

Corollary: We are not only products of the universe but also vital to its meaningful existence, as we are the means by which the universe becomes meaningful and knowledgeable. Without us, there is in a sense no universe, and when we die, we take our knowledge and appreciation of the universe with us. Each of us is essential to the universe in that respect, just as we are essential to each other in our appreciation of each other. Everything that we do in our lives, as long as it makes sense, contributes to the meaningfulness of the universe. All of us are needed to justify the existence of the universe by the meaning we contribute to it. We all are responsible for making our lives as meaningful as possible and have no one to blame but ourselves if we fail to do so.

Fourth Presupposition of Life-Belief

The Contribution of Creativity: We make our lives more purposeful and meaningful by creating new and different things that contribute to the increasing diversity of existence and enrich the universe by our very presence.

Corollary: Exploiting our creativity is essential to the future of humanity. Little or nothing was achievable in the past without the creativity that has been our salvation and our vindication throughout the ages. But it is up to each of us to find our own creative area and achieve the ultimate expression of our individuality. The wealth of artistic creativity is surely worth more to humanity than all the gold, silver and fiat, fake or digital currency circulating throughout the world. Even without money, we would still have art, music, literature, buildings and other means to express ourselves and to find enjoyment in life. In the widest sense, we can all be creative artists of one sort or another. We can all enrich our lives by making the most of our potential artistry. As artists, we can dream up what has never been thought or created before. By putting our dreams into practice, we give them a concrete existence that lasts as long as their materiality persists. But creativity requires the interaction between harmony and conflict.

Fifth Presupposition of Life-Belief

The Maintenance of Harmony: Living beings generally seek out and thrive on harmony. The aim of harmony is to ensure that stability and predictability are maintained. Without a modicum of the latter two conditions, life cannot thrive for long.

Corollary: The main drive of life is towards harmony and the maintenance thereof, but this seldom lasts long. Nothing stays the same over time. Life rarely goes smoothly. Things fall apart all too frequently. Disharmony is also a part of life. Our bodies deteriorate, and our social and personal relationships end in time. Our emotions get in the way and we upset other people, causing discord. We need to destroy to create and kill to eat. We may want everything to stay the same; this is the conservative urge within us all. Unless we can predict with a modicum of certainty, what tomorrow will bring us, our lives are scarcely worth living. Also, the apparent permanence and stability of our surroundings depends on the harmony between the interacting contents of physical objects. Ultimately, harmony depends on the uniformity of nature and on the laws of physics remaining the same. But the harmony of human society and relationships is entirely up to us alone, however badly we manage these.

Sixth Presupposition of Life-Belief

The Imposition of Order: Life is orderly in that its growth and development is guided precisely by DNA, apart from occasional mutations. But throughout its lifetime, the living being strives to impose order on an otherwise disorderly world to ensure its survival and maximise its potential.

Corollary: Chaos and disorder are as evident as any order in the universe. However, despite entropic trends to the contrary, a tiny germ of order is being developed on our minuscule rocky speck at the heart of this unspeakably large universe. Life flourishes by negative entropy in creating order out of disorder. It goes against the dissipating trend of the universe while it lives. We humans, in particular, have the potential to recreate the universe in our own image, but only if we use sufficient intelligence and creativity to harness our abilities to do so.

To some extent, we contribute to the ordering of the universe even by what we do in our daily lives. Even tidying one's home or one's desk creates order that did not exist before. The more order we bring to everything around us the more we become holists who have made a difference by what they do and see things as a whole. Our habits and routines also help us to impose order and discipline on our behaviour.

When we make sense of what we find at the smallest and largest levels of existence, we bring order, meaning and purpose into being. We create order by linking the very large and the very small and making a coherent system of them. We are already doing this with a significant measure of success with the sciences of cosmology, physics, chemistry, biology and the other sciences. In the long run, this increasing orderliness could eventually save the universe from its ultimate fate of total dispersal and heat death.

Seventh Presupposition of Life-Belief

The Resolution of Conflict: Life is full of conflict, dissonance and friction. Its mission is to resolve conflicts since its survival and reproduction depends on it.

Corollary: Life in a sense is an endless fight to exist, survive and propagate itself. A life without conflict or distress of some kind is scarcely conceivable. How we cope with our setbacks and challenges tests our resilience and determination. There are endless problems arising from our conflicting ideas, annoying habits, disagreements, discrepancies, competition with other people and so on. But we strengthen ourselves in resolving these conflicts and the problems arising from them.

War is the worse conflict of all, and our powers of resolution and resilience are tested by it. But we only rid ourselves of war when humanity finally comes together with specific purpose of eliminating conflict between nations. "Nationalism means war!", as Mitterrand said[4], meaning that the nation state stands chiefly in the way of perpetual peace.

The destruction involved in creating new things is unavoidable. Our natural urge for novelty and new things is essential for material progress which is inevitably destructive in paving the way for novelty. Moving forward cannot be done without destroying the status quo in some way. But it is only justifiable if something better is produced in the process.

Eighth Presupposition of Life-Belief

The Benefit of Openness: Life-belief is always open to further thought and development. This is because these presuppositions of life-belief are based on the openness that characterises science at its best.

Corollary: The openness of our beliefs to revision, improvement or cancellation is essential to the progress of humanity. Our minds need to be open to new ways of doing things if we are to improve ourselves materially and morally. We have to be open-minded to reach a clear view of things. In keeping an open mind, we incorporate both sides of an argument perhaps without being aware of it. This helps us to be moderate in our prejudices and pre-occupations, while recognising the alternatives that are always possible. We must learn to be carefully doubtful and when to be cautiously certain.

Being open-minded and forward thinking means that we hold our opinions at arm's length and with some doubt and uncertainty. Open-mindedness is a determination to abandon hypotheses in the face of opposing evidence. An open-minded attitude helps us to treat our conclusions dispassionately so that we don't become unreasonably attached to them. We can then abandon them as soon as the evidence is stacked against them. When they become dominant in our thinking to the extent of explaining anything and everything then our minds are closed to any other way of thinking. There must be limits to the explanatory power of any ideas that occur to us as being true. Believing in life therefore means being open to change for the better without encouraging change for change's sake.

Ninth Presupposition of Life-Belief

The Indispensability of Love: Love is the prime unifying force in the universe. This is not love in the usual sexual or sensual sense but in an interactive sense. It results in things coming together to interact harmoniously. This is love that involves interaction that creates unities and harmonies persisting into the future but not indefinitely. Love makes sense only when it is life giving, life bringing, and life fulfilling.

Corollary: The love of life motivates us in choosing what we do with our lives. We find love not just in our relationships with people and animals but also in the enjoyment of achieving goals and creating things. Love is necessary as a unifying factor that brings us together, but only when it is caring, thoughtful love. Love without sympathy and affection darkens and diminishes our souls especially if it is only lustful love. Whatever we do that benefits others is the essence of love. Thus love, in the widest sense, refers to our reciprocal relationships with each other, society and the universe at large.

Humanity as a whole constitutes the acme of complex loving relationships but only when it looks to the future and attempts to contribute to that future, one way or another. Loving relationships that are confined to the present or rooted in the past are usually selfish and self-centred. Love has no real meaning unless it contributes to future unity and harmony, by producing children or creating buildings, machinery, software, art, music, literature, or anything that is done with loving care or just for the love of it. Love indeed makes the world go around.

Tenth Presupposition of Life-Belief

The Inevitability of Death: Life is not so important that it has to be preserved beyond all reason. Killing people is always to be avoided, and killing animals is only justified by our need to eat and survive. Even vegetarians and vegans have to live off life forms such as plants. Even fruit contains seeds that have the potential of life. Nature itself is prolific in disposing of life through disease, accidents, miscarriages or whatever. Death is an inevitable part of life.

Corollary: Because all human beings are valued individuals, we are not allowed to kill people with impunity. It may be argued that there are exceptions to the rule such as euthanasia, abortion, and the conditions of war, but only the clearest and most generally accepted reasons can justify such exceptions to the rule. We all have to die but it is natural for us to prolong our lives for as long as possible. Life-belief alone encourages us to continue living because of the value and joy of living. Though death and dissolution are ubiquitous and unavoidable, whatever is left behind is not lost as it is available to successors or to whatever incorporates the contents of the defunct living being.

Nothing lasts forever but while it endures, it accumulates unique attributes that enrich the whole after death or dissolution. This is as true of stars as it is of living beings. But the complexity of living beings means that they have more to contribute to their successors after their dissolution. Thus, death has no sting when it contributes to the accumulative trend towards ultimate togetherness that is possible in the future and will be witnessed by posterity but only if we do our best to contribute to that posterity.

When we die we revert to the same state that we were in before we were born. The nothingness following death, an eternity of non-existence, is not to be shunned or hidden behind resurrection fantasies or the like. The more we dread the nothingness of death, the more we value the somethingness of life. The wonderful gift of life is better appreciated when we face up to the ending of life forever when we die.

The Emblematic Heart of Life-Belief
The *Tree of Life* blossoms forth in all directions
while rooted in the universe itself.
The *Key of Life* is the Ankh of ancient Egypt
that opens the door to ever burgeoning life.
Life, Love and Humanity are worth believing in above all.

Part Three

The Principle of Plenitude

In Praise of Plenitude

The aim of life-belief is vivoplenia or fullness of life. The plenary principle of vivoplenia is about making the most of life and are discussed below. Life-belief is complementary to all religions in that the plenary principle offers hope and purpose to everyone, irrespective of their religion or the lack of it. Vivoplenia means getting involved in the world to make it a better place, instead of forsaking it in hope of a better world in the hereafter. Happiness is only achievable within our lifetime and not outside it. Otherwise we are opting out of life and living which is the opposite of vivoplenia. Unless we are full of life we are less than ourselves.

By being full of life, we can strengthen our inner development and make ourselves more fit for the world. We get things done because we are full of the need to do them and are motivated to be up and running. Vivoplenia thereby strengthens our minds against the vicissitudes of life and fortune. It goes beyond all religions in developing a strong mentality or way of thinking that helps us cope with life and make the most of it. Such inner development can override the need for God or a divine being of any kind. A self-sufficiency results that has no need of superstition or invisible presences. It is a state of mind to be learnt by constant practice.

When religious experience is shallow and evanescent, it can be bolstered by a healthy doze of vivoplenia. Typically, religious people get God and feel the comforting presence of God so that they become wonderfully happy and 'saved'. As a result, they no longer feel guilty or despairing. But, in comparison, the life-filled mentality is much more involved and evolved. It is deeper and more self-sustaining. It can cope more easily with sinfulness, guilt, depression or inadequacy, which are kept in perspective and are not overwhelming. There is no thought of doing 'sin' that is harmful to it or to others. The need of god or any spiritual presence palls into insignificance when we are too involved in life and living to feel any need for such things belonging to the past.

Vivoplenia means filling the mind with fruitful thoughts and feelings, and this is a source of moral responsibility. We behave responsibly most of all when we are highly motivated by the enjoyable and worthwhile things that we can do with our lives. Also, by being open to further development and self-fulfilment, our minds become more disciplined and directed in their behaviour. Most mature and responsible people are imbued with vivoplenia even though they don't know it by that name. Thus, moral discipline comes naturally without the need of external imposition. We get to know ourselves thoroughly and learn to live within sensible limits. We are disciplined by self-knowledge of what is good and bad for oneself and what is hurtful to others. This is about depth of character and force of personality. Vivoplenia is also about life-long education. We never stop learning new facts and skills from cradle to grave.

Of course, none of this is exclusive to the plenitude offered by vivoplenia. Religion in general has similar aims. But vivoplenia makes this a matter of internal development instead of external imposition by means of moral rules and clerical supervision. It clarifies what this internal development or self-knowledge is and how it may be achieved, namely, with the help of the overall knowledge offered by Vivodoxia or life belief. That knowledge includes humanist, holist, universalist, prospectivist, and unifying views which are discussed below in Part Four, pages 30 to 54.

Vivoplenia – Being Full of Life

Vivodoxia goes arm-in-arm with *vivoplenia*. Belief in life counts for nothing if it does not contribute to the fullness of our lives – *vivoplenia* – which here means 'full of life'. In a vivopleniary frame of mind we believe in the fullness of life and in everything it has to offer. This frame of mind is common to countless people, and this simply gives name to it in the context of life which is the sphere that encompasses all other spheres since we have only *one* life to make the most of. Vivoplenia is also helps us to fill a void that may otherwise engulf us and make life seem pointless.

Reasons for Living. To make the most of our lives, we need as many reasons for living as we can think of.   They can help us to strengthen our resolve to live as well and as fully as we are physically capable of doing. We may have reasons for living of which we are not fully aware or which we don't put into words. We may even deny that we need any reasons for living but that usually means that we can't think of them or bring them to mind or that we find our present ones to be inadequate or unconvincing. Much more about our reasons for living can be found in my book, *The Will to Live: A Systematic Guide to our Reasons for Living* (Almostic Publications 2015). See also pages 22-23 below.

Being Full of Life. To be full of life is to be dualistically active and passive within the sphere of life. What this means is as follows. Living beings are both active and passive. Sometimes they are more active than they are passive, and sometimes they are more passive than active. Non-life is either totally active or totally passive and there is no middle ground. Thus, the principle of life and living is a dualist contrast between activity and passivity. But life itself is divided into beings that are mainly either more active or more passive in their activity. This applies especially to the division between animals and plants; but also to animals that are mainly either carnivorous or herbivorous in their consumption of food: the former are usually active and the latter usually passive.

Human beings are more indefinitely both active and passive than other animals. We move more frequently and freely from the one to the other than other animals. We can be indolent at times and hyperactive at other times. This indefinite oscillation is governed by internal purposes rather than by mechanistic determinism. To do or not to do, is the perennial point of indecision. It is important never to be entirely sure whether doing anything is the right thing to do. This is the essence of open-mindedness which characterises life-belief at its best.

Factual belief betters spiritual belief. Our factual beliefs give us depth in thought and feeling that is more lasting than spiritual beliefs which are all too often based more on sentiment than on evidence. Factual beliefs are based on the realities around us, and we can rely on them long term, unlike spiritual beliefs which can be short term and evanescent.

Facts concern what really happens, what is really done, what people really do, and how people really are. In my book, *Jesus of Nazareth: The Real Man and his Message* (Almostic Publications, 2019). I work out from the available evidence who Jesus really was and what he was really like. In so far as the Gospels contain believable facts, we can accept his real existence, but they contain stories that are not believable facts. For example, in a transfiguration story, Jesus leads Peter, John and James up a high mountain and he seemingly talks to the prophets Elijah and Moses (Mark 9:2 to 9:13). This is surely a dream sequence which these disciples collectively persuaded themselves to believe in as fact. It is too unbelievable to be anything else but a dream, perhaps induced by drugs or the rarified air of a 'high mountain'. True believers believe in such stories as being divinely inspired which is the essence of spiritual belief that underscores most if not all religions.

It is not easy to face the hard facts of life and not be intimidated by them. In response we are prone to escape into fantasies and obsessions that are more pleasing to us. But we bolster our self-confidence and strength of character when we face facts and avoid fantasies. It is weakness of mind and character that makes us run away from harsh realities. To do something that is hard to do is satisfying and rewarding in itself. Otherwise, we would not have athletes and sportspersons who gain satisfaction from their relentless dedication to their sport and all the difficulties involved.

When the factual realities of life and humanity are evidentially based, they are more generally agreed across humanity than religious beliefs. This applies particularly to the facts of science that are universally applied throughout the world. Vastly more people put these facts into practice than there are adherents of any religion. More people in the sciences, medical science and education have confidence in these facts than there are those having confidence in any religion. Indeed, many religious people regard science as a form of religion though it is far more open to revision and updating than any religion that is sincerely believed in.

Believing in the fact of life is not the same as believing in the spirit of life. The former is more fundamental and important than the latter. The spirit of life is an insubstantial feeling, while believing in the fact is more reliable and long-lasting. It is within the fact of life that we can build our vivoplenia by finding out more about life and the possibilities that it offers. There is no limit to what we can do with our lives if we put our minds to it.

We have only one life to live unless we can believe in an afterlife of some kind. The default position is that life is all there is and that death simply brings it to a complete end. Fortunate is the person who has faith enough to believe in an afterlife but without this, we can nevertheless have faith in life and humanity as reinforcing *vivodoxia* with *vivoplenia* can be sufficient to make life worth living.

Vivoplenia is a philosophical stance. It invites thinking about all aspects of the human spirit instead of confining it in favour of an orthodoxy to which we must conform without question. We thereby stimulate thinking about beliefs of all kinds. It is a dualist view that is concerned about both sides of an argument and never about imposing one argument on everyone.

The *Plenitude Principles* may be summarised as follows:

1. *Vivoplenia* is all about making the most of life as a whole because it is a gift to be savoured, enjoyed and propagated. As the word means 'fullness of life', it involves living life to the full.

2. *Vivoplenia* is not a religion but a philosophy or way of living. Life is essentially to be lived to the full. But we cannot live it to the full unless we have developed ourselves inwardly rather than superficially.

3. *Vivoplenia* involves believing in what life has to offer. Unless we believe in life and its possibilities we cannot make the most of it. If we are negative about life, it loses meaning and value to us.

4. *Vivoplenia* constitutes a *prime principle of life* that puts as much as possible into life and living. But this can only be done by taking the bad with the good and by balancing the extremes to which we are prone too often in the course of our lives.

The Role of Sublimation. Life is made fuller and more creative by sublimation. Practising restraint in sexual matters strengthens the soul in the fight to live life to the full. Great energy is released by such restraint and in disciplining our sexual impulses. Moreover, wise men and also Holy Scriptures throughout the ages have attested to the weakening and stupefying effects of sexual indulgence, though sexologists in these declining times seem not to agree with that. Admittedly, sexual restraint must be applied with restraint, lest the energy is diverted in unhealthy, harmful or illegal directions. Sexual repression is only productive if it is applied wisely and thoughtfully; hence the need for sagacity.

The Plenitude of Sagacity. Only the wise can truthfully claim to be full of life. Foolish people waste their time doing harmful things that do not become them or do not make them feel any better. We want more of life but only wisdom can ensure a wholesome life. Wisdom enables us to embrace more and appreciate more than otherwise, as it gives us the self-knowledge to see more clearly what truly benefits us. It means doing fulfilling things that make life more pleasant and tolerable. It involves self-discipline and the rewards of wisdom make it worth pursuing. Wise people are constantly conscious of the adverse consequences of pointless behaviour. Acquiring wisdom involves changing minds and living in a better way. Fashionable opinions about how we think about things may need to be challenged. We are not necessarily determined in our behaviour either by our genes or our upbringing. It may be hard to do but we can choose to change our ways of thinking and behaving when we find them deficient or uncongenial. Giving up cigarette smoking is something that many people do successfully, and they feel the better for it. We can be wise people because we choose to be and not because we are meant to be. There is more about the importance of sagacity in my book of that name – *Sagacity: The Way to Wisdom* (Almostic Publications, 2019).

Exemplary human beings. Wisdom is seen in practice in the lives of exemplary human beings such as Moses, Jesus Christ, The Buddha, Confucius, Zoroaster, and Mohammed. Such individuals are exemplary teachers from whom we have much to learn. They are examples to us of what can be achieved spiritually in developing our inner being (as defined below p. 25). But they were no more than human beings and it is inhuman to make more of them by deifying or exalting them in any extravagant way. They may be exemplary individuals but being human means that they were as flawed as we all are. We have a right to criticise them for their shortcomings as much as the rest of us are subject to criticism. Ultimately, their respective messages are more important than what they were as persons. It is entirely up to us all to make the effort and to impose the discipline required to achieve the wisdom exemplified by these individuals.

The Light of Life. The more we do with our lives, the more we pour light on life. By being a shining example to others, we become luminaries who are beacons of the coming future in which everything will be sorted out. Thus, the purpose of vivoplenian illumination is to enlighten and enrich our lives and enable us to see them more acutely and accurately than before. The way that we work this out makes us what we are as unique beings. We become luminaries who shed light each in our own way. The luminary therefore takes pride in shining a light on life. Light is after all the mainstay of the universe which came into being with a blaze of light that is still with us to this day. Shining a light on things is looking on the bright side of life. It makes us cheerful and optimistic so that our company is a delight to others. When brought into the light, everything makes more sense and is more endurable than otherwise. The luminary therefore aspires to enlighten everything and everyone with the light of knowledge and understanding. In this context, we learn to like what we see in ourselves so that others can also like what they see in us.

The expected result is a *Sinclarity* in which we are clear about what life is all about. Enlightenment is the Sinclarist goal: Sinclair – St. Clair – Sanctus Clarus – The Holy Light – Enlightenment – Illuminismo – Éclaircissement – Aufklärung. A state of enlightenment is the aim of my book: *The Way of Togetherness: Hope for the Future in a Godless World* (Almostic Publications, 2019). If religion is to have a future it must involve our coming together to enlighten our respective communities and take them forward to a better future, which is discussed below in Part Six.

Wisdom and Self-Improvement

The inner development of vivoplenia therefore makes for wisdom and self-improvement. By becoming more inwardly aware of ourselves and our strengths and weaknesses, we become wiser and more considerate persons who are more one with ourselves and the world. My *Sagacity* book discusses the sagacious state of mind through the headings of sagacity, reality, reciprocity, morality, equanimity and tranquillity. It is therefore a valuable contribution to the thinking behind life-belief and vivoplenia.

The Importance of Wisdom. Wisdom is in short supply these days. Its scarcity allows unwisdom to flourish. We are plagued with the unwise acts perpetrated by unwise leaders, crooked businessmen, delinquent bankers, perverted priests, lying politicians, randy entertainers, and so on. A surfeit of selfishness and self indulgence underlies this unwisdom; a surfeit that strangles at birth the wisdom of experience. The lack of insight, hindsight and foresight means that not enough thought is put into what is done. Too many leaders are motivated by populism, nationalism and other 'isms' that overlook the common good of humanity which has always been the chief concern of the wise men of old.

A healthy dose of self-improvement is needed to counter the selfishness and self satisfaction that prevails so much today. People are not improving themselves when they go to extremes in search of enjoyment for its own sake. Opiates, alcohol, eating disorders, sex addiction are among the excesses and extremes to which they are driven in a culture that gives them no boundaries to what they can or cannot do. Also, as a species, we need to get wise to what is good for us in the long term. We can better save the planet by living wisely and by using our resources more wisely and thoughtfully.

The way to wisdom involves self-improvement, and this means widening our outlooks, firstly by education and then by looking at the bigger picture, improving our attitudes by avoiding extremes, rectifying our moral lapses by the control of feelings and emotions, and finding peace and tranquillity by getting in tune with the universe. Wisdom also involves knowing ourselves and our strengths and weaknesses. Such self-knowledge helps us to face up to realities and constantly seek the truth. Being a dynamic species, we need to keep moving forward if we are to get anywhere, and self-improvement is the motive power by which we do so.

But is there any point in being wise if there is no reward for it? The most unwise of people are often lauded and rewarded in spite of, and even because of, their ignorance and bad behaviour. Nevertheless, it can be said that wisdom, and good behaviour generally, has its own reward. Peace of mind, wholeness of character, at-one-ness with the world, and contentment with ourselves and the way that our lives are unfolding – these are among the rewards that make a good and wise life worth living when such a life is sincerely led. Also, the peace and harmony of the world may be enhanced by the wisdom of the many, whereas these are destroyed when selfishness and immorality prevail.

Rationalising our Passions. We ought to be passionately involved in life; not just any passions but those rational passions that take us forward to better things. This includes the rational passions for truth, honesty, clarity, evidence, consistency, respect and sympathy. A strong feeling for these confirms our wisdom and enhances our self-improvement. These passions are our best bulwark against the extremist state of mind since they make open-mindedness a matter of passionate concern and not something which is merely desirable in an objective, offhand manner. Rationalising them fosters open-mindedness by opening the mind to different ways of thinking. They basically express the ordinary person's common-sense view of things. Those who willingly maintain an open, friendly and guileless approach to life, will sympathise with and apply the rational passions without needing to think too deeply about them. There is more about the value of rational passions in my book, *The Way of Togetherness* (Almostic Publications, 2018) pages 47-52.

The Will to Live

Vivoplenia means finding reasons within ourselves to survive, strive and thrive throughout our lives. This is the subject of my book *The Will to Live: A Systematic Guide to our Reasons for Living* (Almostic Publications, 2014). This is a particularly successful book and is still selling well. The will to live is an important topic as it is common to all life-forms. Life distinguishes itself above all by its will to live. Survival is not enough, as there is always something within the individual life-form that motivates and drives it to make as much of its life as possible. This is where the will comes from – the inner drive to do things. The more internally developed, the more the will is built up and strengthened. Thus, the plenary strength within each living being impels them forward in live out their lives, and it empowers their will to live.

The will to live is particularly important for human beings, as we have each to work out for ourselves what our lives are all about, unlike other animals that are more subject to genetic influences. The will makes our lives worth living and keeps us going when the going gets tough. It is the inner strength we summon up when we really need it. It acts as a unifying power within us that helps us to continue living in spite of all difficulties we face. Our strength of purpose depends on our inner will keeping us together. We don't need artificial stimulants to keep us going if the will to live is sufficiently strong. All those film stars, rock stars and celebrities, who have died young through overdoses or over-indulgence of some kind, lacked sufficient will to keep going. They needed drugs, drink or whatever as they couldn't face life without them. They couldn't live quietly with themselves from day-to-day as they lacked enough in them to make them at ease with themselves. Their moods got the better of them as they had no control over their feelings. If the will to live is sufficiently strong and well-developed, we need no more than our own inner resources to make life worthwhile. We strengthen our inner being and become more spirited.

Those who lack the will to live may contemplate suicide, if not commit it. They may even regard their lives as so worthless that they kill other people whose lives they regard as equally worthless. Mass killers have given up on life entirely; therefore, they wish to deprive as many people as possible of the privilege of living. To combat such negativity, we need reasons for living that enhance the value of our lives. The more reasons we have, the stronger our will to live for the best possible purposes. The active search for reasons for living helps us to develop the will within us, and there is much we can do to aid its development, as my book *The Will to Live* shows.

Our sustained enjoyment of life is based in our will or inner being. When we cease enjoying the simple, everyday things in life such as going to work, watching television, participating in sport, video games and so on, life can lose its lustre. We can only look within ourselves and find more and better reasons for living. By opening our minds to the opportunities before us, we can think our way out of such existential emptiness. One way of doing this is to consult the range of possibilities available to us, and the content of the *Will to Live* book may be helpful in that regard.

To make the most of our lives, we need as many reasons for living that we can think of. They can help us to strengthen our resolve to live as well and as fully as we are physically capable of doing. We may have reasons for living which we are not fully aware of or which we don't put into words. We may even deny that we have any reasons for living but that usually means that we can't think of them or bring them to mind or that we find our present ones to be inadequate or unconvincing.

A large range of choices are mentioned in my *The Will to* Live, but they are not meant to be rigorously compatible with each other. The fact that they are mentioned in the book does not mean that I personally condone or approve of them as choices. It is merely pointed out that people have made such choices in the past and no doubt will do so in the future. They think that they have valid or worthwhile reasons for making such choices, or they may have no reasons at all, and do so for a whim, a laugh or whatever.

The Importance of Atheism

Belief in the existence of God is not incompatible with life-belief. It is still possible to have both god-belief and life-belief. But belief in the existence of God is not necessary to life-belief, as is argued throughout this book. It also is essential that religious people understand atheism and appreciate the view that the universe can be explained without reference to a god or creator. Otherwise, they will make too much of God and expect too much of their belief in the notion. They may go to the extremes of killing or disparaging people because they believe that it is in God's interests to do so. Life is paramount and only the primacy of life-belief reflects this view unequivocally. This book is therefore about using science to broaden minds and moderate religious beliefs of any kind.

The Compatibility of Atheism

A belief in the existence of God is compatible with life-belief but is not necessary to it; such a belief is personal to those who believe in God. Some religions are not based on god belief or have many gods. Atheists can readily embrace life-belief as it does not imply belief in the existence of any god or gods. The atheist is only required to appreciate life and the value of living generally. This ensures the inclusivity of life-belief but it is still possible to be negative about life and to deny its value for whatever perverse reason. Even having a negative opinion about life is still a part of life and living which itself cannot be denied. Also, the denial of religion altogether is still compatible with life-belief since it is an opinion about efficacy of an aspect of life. However, a hatred of humanity is tantamount to misanthropy, and it is difficult to reconcile such hatred with life-belief which is nothing without our accepting people and all their faults and limitations. The idea of God hasn't been good for humanity as god-believers are still killing people and maligning each other in the name of God and their respective religions. So far from unifying humanity, God has driven us apart. Life-belief could hardily be less successful in bringing humanity together.

The Atheist's Creed

The Fact of Life and Act of Living are more important to me than anything material. I am suffused with life and living, and I appreciate above all the Gift of Life and the Love of Living. Life is the great gift given me by the workings of the universe. My idea of that gift is therefore based on scientific facts concerning the workings of the universe and not on any divine or spiritual fantasies. These workings made it possible for my parents to conceive me and bring me up as best they could. My love of life enables me to choose what I do with it. I am grateful to the material universe for giving me all the opportunities for enjoyment and fulfilment during my brief span of existence on this planet.

Life is Self-Sustaining

Science tells that life is self-sustaining and needs no external influences. Each life-form develops inwardly by interacting with its environment and by building up its internal complexity over time. This internal activity is here called 'inner being'. It is an entirely physical process that is not spiritual or non-material in any way. The phrase 'inner being' is preferred over non-material words such as 'mind', 'spirit' and 'soul' which are assumed to exist as substances apart from the physical activity of the brain and body. 'Inner being' refers to the processes occurring in the brain and body that make possible our self-identity and subjectivity. These unifying processes make possible the 'I', 'self' or 'ego'. Inner being underlies our consciousness in which we are aware of what we are doing and what is happening to us, even in our dreams.

Inner being is not an occult, spiritual entity or a substance of any kind. It is entirely explicable in concrete, physical terms, namely, in a complex inversion theory of brain workings. Inner being exists in living beings because their physical activity in brain became more complexified than in less complex physical objects. It results from the complexification of physical activity in brain and body which is sufficient to produce self-identity and consciousness by referring back into itself. Self-reference is therefore the key to understanding how we become aware of ourselves as being distinct from our surroundings and our own feelings. Subjective awareness may be objectively considered as resulting from the turning in or invagination of highly complex neural activity which is wholly physical.

Neural brain workings are therefore no less the author of self-identity.

These workings transcend the normal physical activity of which it is composed because of the complexification and self-reference involved in these workings. The nature of these physical workings is what is meant by 'inner being'.

The theory is that consciousness results from the complex unification of neural activity as it moves around the brain and central nervous system. Inner being comes together and turns into itself to form this mobile unity. This is the source of our subjective experiences which we think of as being experienced by ourselves alone. We are aware of our subjective existence because this complex physical activity in the brain and central nervous system turns into itself to make self awareness possible. Whether we call it the 'I', 'self' or 'ego', it exists because of that complex physical activity. The subject of 'inner being' is also discussed at length in pages 8 to 28 of *The Way of Togetherness* book. The account of 'inner being' there is mainly about the self-referential nature of inner being. It is a process that refers back into itself to create self-identity and consciousness.

We may speculate that the turning in or inversion of inner being becomes a spiral that reaches down to the level of sub-atomic quantum level. There it partakes of the indeterminacy of that region and this is the source of our freewill and serendipitous creativity. The complexification results in a transcendent unity in which the whole becomes more than its parts. The transcendence reaches the quantum area where indeterminacy makes free will possible. We are not determined by the physical activity in our brains because there is sufficient indeterminacy to make our thinking indefinite and creative. Subjectivity is therefore transcendent, self referential, as well as highly complexified.

The theory therefore implies that neural activity comes together, turns into itself at a unified point and then spirals down to the quantum level where inner being uses the indeterminacy of freewill, in which our thoughts, ideas and images are experienced subjectively. At this unified point, inner being or the ego universalizes itself and connects with the universe as a whole within the quantum field of existence.

In this view, consciousness is explained as a process that reaches down into the quantum area of existence and interacts with it. It is still completely physical in its workings. There is interaction with the quantum area but clearly it is not all taking place at that level. The quantum area can't do anything since it is indeterminate and neither here nor there. The processes of the autonomic nervous system are therefore highly complex interactions that transcend their physicality in interacting at the quantum level of existence.

Thus, life is self-sustaining in that its processes can be explained in terms of its internal activity and there is no need for external explanations. For example, the cells in our bodies are not under our conscious control.

They are tiny independent factories that produce enzymes and hormones while interacting with each other in very complex ways. Their internal functioning is governed by molecules such as DNA and RNA. These are highly complex molecules that emerged by evolutionary processes in the course of time. They were created by no more than the complexifying processes of evolution. Such complexified processes and their transcendent interactions are surely enough to explain how life functions and how it has come into being through aeons of complexification over long periods of time. Thus, we must think in terms of deep time.

The Role of Time

All things are possible over time. Life needs time to come to fruition. When the religious mindset is narrowed down by scriptural teaching, it lacks an appreciation of 'deep time', which is an understanding of how complex life emerges over eons of time without divine intervention. The universe is about 13.8 billion years old, and it took 300 million years after its beginning for the basic elements to complexify and produce carbon, oxygen and other heavy elements. Some 9 billion years later the Earth was formed and the earliest life-forms began to emerge. But it was another 3 billion years before the first multi-cellular organisms emerged (about 610 million years ago). Amphibian animals emerged only 300 million years after that. And it has taken another 300 million years for human beings to appear on Earth. It takes so much time that there is no need for external intervention. Life does it all by itself and takes its time. It is a matter of understanding what this complexity really consists of, and it is here that quantum activity may be involved and ultimately quantum consciousness. This is the root of our freedom of will despite all the mechanistic and biological determinisms to which we are otherwise subject. But this is all imaginative speculation at a philosophical level and it means that there are still known unknowns aplenty for us to speculate about.

The Self-Generation of Life

It is an astonishing fact that we all began as a single fertilised cell - mere speck that was barely visible to the human eye. But that tiny cell had all the information it needed to multiply and eventually become the complex entity that each one of us is. The cell did not need any external intervention but only a congenial environment and enough nourishment to grow into what it was destined to become by its genetic inheritance. It began by multiplying all by itself into an embryo which at first closely resembles the embryos of many other animals, as this 19th century diagram shows:[5]

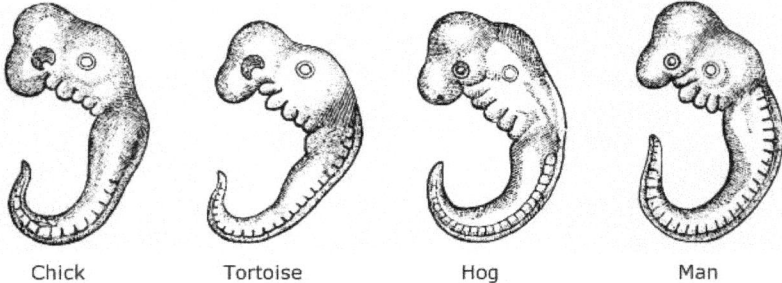

| Chick | Tortoise | Hog | Man |

Four Different Species of Embryos

All viable life-forms develop thus by means of their inner resources while interacting with their environment and being adequately nourished as they grow. We have no personal knowledge or awareness of our undergoing such an embryonic development, yet science clearly tells us that this is so. The evidence for this is overwhelming and undeniable by any reasonable person. Science is needed to help us understand what life is all about – how it came about – its nature and its persistence in all kinds of environment. This knowledge can only increase our wonder at the self-sustaining resilience of life. The purpose of this book is to make this view plain to the most religious of individuals.

A Hymn in Praise of Life
(A Fragment)
I sing in praise of a long and happy life.
Though our lives be marred by worry and strife
Still we can make the best of what is given
But only when for a full life we have striven
We can on Earth find no nobler cause
Governed as we are by physical laws
That have made us what we are
And even yet in life we can go far
But we must make good our past
And only do the things that last
Mending the Earth as we go and venture
To the stars and beyond where life must endure.

Part Four

Strengthening Life-Belief

The Build-Up of Life-Belief

Life-belief or Vivodoxia is strengthened by humanist, holist, universalist, prospectivist, and unifying views as outlined below. All these aspects are potentially compatible with religions in general.

Life-belief is humanist in being concerned about the welfare of human beings and their place in the universe.

It is holist as it looks at life as a whole and life makes most sense when seen from a distance.

It is universalist in seeing life as an intimate part of the universe in which it has its part to play.

 It has a prospectivist view which looks forward to the future of life on this planet and elsewhere.

It aims to unify humanity along the lines of the comparative religion movement of the twentieth century.

The point is made here that all these aspects should be taken account of in every religion. They can often be found somewhere in their respective scriptures and religious practices. Whenever they show respect for life and humanity, they are fo llowing the Vivodoxian way, either implicitly or explicitly.

In this book, it is argued consistently and repetitiously that our future as a unified species necessitates that we move forward together. To do so, we must stress what we have in common more than what divides us.[5] This is particularly the case concerning our place in the universe. The Vivodoxian view looks at us in an overall universal context. It supplies what is often deficient or overlooked in most religions, namely, the context in which they exist, as opposed to their customary stand-alone context.

Firstly, the humanist view is itself an inclusive belief system in that religious people also behave mostly in humanist ways. Only fanatics and hot-heads are inhuman in imposing their views on others. Religions would have more in common if their adherents were explicitly to adopt the humanist view that places great value on the individual human being. However, in their view, humanism is too centred on the human being, whereas there is much more to the universe than mere human beings. For them, there has to be a superior, omniscient being to whom everything is known and has no 'unknown unknowns' or things that never can be known. Yet only intelligent beings, such as ourselves, can get to know what was previously unknown. When knowledge is revealed to us, an external source for it is not required as it is generated entirely within us. This is all the explanation we need. Anything else is more imagined than real. It is insulting to geniuses, artists and inventive people to attribute their ingenuity to a god or spirit of some kind. It is only wishful thinking to believe that anything else than human ingenuity is involved.

Yet the traditional religions seek to transcend humanity and humble us in the face of greater things such as god, aliens, angels, prophets, gurus or whatever is exulted in any particular religion. But such transcendence is achieved in life-belief through the views of holism, universalism, prospectivism and unity as expounded in this book.

Secondly, the holist view looks at life and humanity from the overall perspective. The most transcendent of religions is often not holist enough as it fails to take in many perspectives, especially that of science. Nor does Christianity take in the perspective of Judaism, Islam, Hinduism and other religions. And the same applies to all the religions in respect of other religions. Only vivodoxia is receptive to the perspective of all religions and is therefore genuinely holist, since they are stand-alone doctrines that are true to themselves alone.

Thirdly, the universalist view considers our place in the universe. That view goes beyond religions in general because they are so rooted in the past. Universalism itself is transcendental as it means that there is more to anything than the sum of its parts. This wholeness gives us our transcendence. From the universal viewpoint, we are always capable of much more than sum-total of opportunities before us. Vivodoxia seeks to maximise these opportunities by releasing people from the artificial, rigid restraints imposed by religion to differentiate its adherents from people who are not of the same faith.

Fourthly, prospectivism encourages us to look to the future and to consider carefully the effects of our present actions on prosperity. We must judge our actions by the tribunal of future generations. Wars and conflicts contribute nothing of lasting value to posterity. They contribute only to the history of human folly. Religion in general is more concerned with recreating the past in the present than in preparing us for a better future. It needs the prospectivist perspective to make it face the needs of the future.

Fifthly, the unifying view brings us all together in relation to our evolutionary position in the universe. We are inwardly highly complex beings, and that complexity has transcendent effects. It makes us endlessly creative and imaginative beings. Humanity also contributes to the possible evolutionary advance towards a unifying point in the future. It is easy to think of this unifying point as being a god or divine being in some way but this is an unnecessary inference. Any being visualised as superior to us in intelligence and its technological advances can be regarded as 'divine' if we so wish, especially if we want to think of them as having some kind of unknown, arcane influence on us and our affairs. In the absence of convincing evidence, it is all imaginative invention which is already well explored in science fiction films such as 'The Matrix' (1999, 2003) and 'Transcendence' (2014).

The Humanist View

Modern humanism owes much to Christianity. Indeed humanism can be regarded as a non-religious successor to Christianity, which recognised the value of human beings at the beginning, though Christians have not always practised what they preached in their persecution of heretics and unbelievers in subsequent centuries. Nevertheless, the Christian religion made a considerable advance in repudiating the *Lex Talionis* – the 'eye for an eye' doctrine.

Repudiation of the Lex Talionis. This is the law of retaliation – the Latin means literally 'the law of the claw'. The repudiation of vengeance for vengeance's sake was part of the teachings attributed to Jesus of Nazareth. He was particularly humanistic in his tolerance of opposing opinions as well as in his emphatic repudiation of the *Lex Talionis* – the law of vengeance – an eye for an eye. The propagation of this view is one of Christianity's greatest contributions to human advancement. All religions would benefit from the explicit repudiation of this law.

In that regard, humanism has taken on the Christian repudiation of the *Lex Talionis* of the *Old Testament*. The obnoxious law appears there three times: *Exodus* 21:23-25; *Leviticus* 24:19, 20; *Deuteronomy* 19:21. "If any harm follows, then you shall give life for life, eye for eye, tooth for tooth, hand for hand, foot for foot, burn for burn, wound for wound, stripe for stripe." The *Lex Talionis* is very ancient as it appears in the earliest known code of laws, the Code of Hammurabi, the ruler of Babylon from c.2285 to c.2242 BC:

> 196. If a man put out the eye of another man, his eye shall be put out. [An eye for an eye]
> 197. If he break another man's bone, his bone shall be broken.
> 198. If he put out the eye of a freed man, or break the bone of a freed man, he shall pay one gold mina.
> 199. If he put out the eye of a man's slave, or break the bone of a man's slave, he shall pay one-half of its value.
> 200. If a man knock out the teeth of his equal, his teeth shall be knocked out. [A tooth for a tooth]
> 201. If he knock out the teeth of a freed man, he shall pay one-third of a gold mina.[6]

The principle is clear and apparently simple: if a man has inflicted an injury on any person, an equivalent injury shall be inflicted upon him. In the ancient context, it was a merciful ruling since the aim was to limit the extent of vengeance. No more than an eye for eye was allowed by the law. But Jesus of Nazareth objected to the very principle of that law because retaliation, however controlled and restricted, had no place in his thinking:

> "You have heard that it was said, 'Eye for eye, and tooth for tooth.' But I tell you, do not resist an evil person. If someone strikes you on the right cheek, turn to him the other also. And if someone wants to sue you and take your tunic, let him have your cloak as well. If someone forces you to go one mile, go with him two miles. Give to the one who asks you, and do not turn away from the one who wants to borrow from you." (*Matthew* 5:38-42)

This kind of forbearance was a great advance in ethical thinking. Those religions that have not seriously taken this humanistic view on-board are to this day causing wars and violence in some parts of the world. For example, the Middle East has experienced decades of senseless wars and conflict because of tit-for-tat vengeance between one nation or faction and another. One side bombs the other side and immediately the other side retaliates by bombing in equal measure. Contrast that senseless, inhumane behaviour with the British response to the IRA bombing activities in mainland Britain during the 1970s and 80s. Retaliation was never considered either by the public or the UK Government. Dublin or West Belfast or Londonderry might have been bombed in retaliation for such atrocities on the mainland. But this was never seriously considered by any sensible person. Yet this is exactly what has happened in those Middle East countries that have never adopted the Christian view of forbearance in the face of violence and provocation. Perhaps we will never see lasting peace in such countries until this Christian view prevails in a renewed Vivodoxian world that places total value on human life.

The Holist View

Religious people can benefit from adopting the holist view as it gives them the widest possible view of the place of their religion in the scheme of things. They can then see themselves as being a part of the whole instead of the be-all and end-all. Their religion can't be the answer to all problems everywhere; otherwise that one religion would be accepted and into practice by everyone without exception. The overall view enables them to see their limitations. Within that view they make a valid contribution to humanity instead of being forced uncritically on everyone.

The word 'holon' is based on the Greek 'holos' meaning 'whole'. It refers an overall, holist view that is expressed even in everyday speech by words such as idea, concept, notion, meme, cultural artefact, or whatever. The holon can be dynamic or static in its usage. Static holons, like 'communism', are absolute and changeless, and are characteristic of authoritarian regimes, ideologies, religions, and of extremist thinking in general. The dynamic holon is open-ended, changeable and adaptable. Scientific holons, such as atomic particles, are often dynamic in that sense, since their properties are open to further discussion, research or experimentation. Dynamic holons are therefore interactive in that they are subject to changing circumstances to which they respond and adapt. Thus the avoidance of extremism, bigotry and tyranny depends on the use of dynamic as opposed to static holons.

Looking at things as a whole is a holist view unique to human beings. We are the only *holist* species on this planet, as we alone can look at things as a whole, as long as we make up our minds to do so. Other animals are too rooted in the here-and-now to see the bigger picture. They are more governed by instinct and present exigencies than we are, as we can learn by upbringing and education to be more than merely instinctive or impulsive creatures. Thus, the holist view is not acquired by instinct; we learn it by education and experience.

We learn to form conceptions of things and gradually learn to see that things are grouped together into wholes. Houses are brought together to form towns; towns and cities form countries, and countries form the whole world. Our conceptions grow to form bigger wholes. Thus, our conceptualising abilities enable us to see things as a whole. The more conceptions that we include in our thinking, the more holist we are. But if a particular religion is a person's whole world, then a lot is missed out, and they may be accused of narrow-mindedness. In the holist view, we can conceive of everything being connected together around a centralising point which is our own thinking about things. This point may be called the holon. It is being constantly being formed and reformed to make our holist view dynamic and fluid in relation to changing realities. How we can achieve this holist frame of mind is outlined here.

The dynamic holist view is incompatible with extremism of any kind. The extremist typically focuses on one view to the exclusion of all others. Anyone taking the whole view cannot regard one view to be the whole truth of the matter unless its merits and demerits are seen in relation to opposing views. The holist view combats extremism by incorporating and appreciating opposing points of view. Unlike extremism which is narrowly focused on one point of view, the holist view faces the problem of discriminating or judging between opposing points of view. It enables us to step outside them, and it facilitates decisiveness as to which is to be preferred.

Thus, anyone who is not holist minded can be vulnerable to extremism. A good test of whether a person is vulnerable to an extremist mentality is to ascertain the extent of their broadmindedness and openness to alternative ways of thinking. They must admit the vulnerability of their beliefs and the possibility of their being wrong or not having considered the whole truth of the matter.

In practice, both science and religion fail to look at things as a whole. When their concerns are too narrow and inward-looking, they cannot give us the whole picture. At their extremes, science can be too specialised and reductionist, and religion can be too otherworldly and rooted in narrow beliefs. The holist view helps us to avoid scientific specialisation and reductionism on the one hand, and religious unworldliness and credulity on the other hand. It is not a specialised or reductionist view as it is all-embracing and all-encompassing. It is not unworldly and credulous as it takes us into the real world while expecting us to do our best as individuals and make the world a better place in which to live in and prosper.

Holism gives us an informed wisdom that is ever open to continuous development in the light of further thought, experience and information. It gives substance to the practical kind of wisdom characteristic of wise men down the ages. It is therefore a philosophy to be taught and understood; it is not in itself a religion to be preached or believed in uncritically.

From the holist viewpoint we can ascertain the extent of our ignorance of things. We can't do anything about our lack of knowledge and understanding unless we see the full extent of our deficiencies. What we do not know can never be grasped without stepping outside ourselves and broadening our imaginations in that way.

Holism takes account of all points of view without promoting any single viewpoint as being the answer to everything. It is about inclusivity as compared with the exclusivity of religions, ideologies and other narrow ways of thinking. It is therefore a philosophy which involves thinking about things critically and carefully. The consistent holist can never be a single-minded demagogue or charlatan enforcing his views on other people. He can only be a teacher and never a preacher.

Moreover, the holist view does not reduce the individual to the whole. On the contrary, it is suffused with the Autonomy Principle which states that each individual is an autonomous person capable of unique and irreplaceable development. We are all ends in ourselves, and the role of society is to provide the framework in which our ends can be achieved. The holist view therefore works from the individual upwards by ensuring that each person adopts that view for their own ends and not because it is imposed from above *ex cathedra.*

Holism is nothing if it is not comprehensive. It is an amalgam or plethora of 'isms' that include not just holism but also humanism, dualism, interactivism, emergentism, centralism, vitalism, mentalism, to name but a few. In all these areas of thought, holist view is open to further development and restatement. In pursuit of truth, criticisms are ever welcome, as it recedes rainbow-like ever before us and demands constant work to keep up with it, in the light of further experience and knowledge. Firstly, there is the *internal* problem of balancing all these points of view and dealing with inconsistencies and contradictions. Secondly, there is the *external* problem of constantly relating the material to external reality and refining it accordingly. There is no end to this process of reconciling these internal and external aspects and this is only a beginning.

In this view, the problem of relating ourselves to the world becomes a holist problem involving ourselves alone. We need not look to non-human intervention for comfort or solace as our problem arise within us. They are solvable by seeing ourselves as an intimate part of the whole picture and by harmonising ourselves with the world as a whole so that we become at one with it. We achieve atonement (at-one-ment) in that way. Atheism is the logical consequence of forgetting about God or any external being superior to us because we have no further need for it. But, nevertheless, atheists can respect the need of others to believe in the existence of God when that belief is a sustaining and inspiring thing without which they may consider themselves to be lost.

The Universalist View

Whereas holism is about including everything at a factual level, universalism is about our feelings and thoughts concerning our place in the universe. Universalism involves passionate belief in the possibilities facing the human race. It is perhaps the highest and purest of all beliefs, and all faiths are strengthened by acknowledging the value of these possibilities. This is a universalising as well as a holist exercise as it highlights the role of humanity in the universe as a whole. As we are capable of contemplating the universe as a whole, we are a more important part of it than other living species that are incapable of such contemplation.

Justifying faith in our future possibilities is a high endeavour worthy of us all. It takes courage to believe in this against all the cynicism and scepticism to which the decadent élite of the Western World subscribes so fashionably. But this courage is sustainable by the use of reason and wise acts; by continually seeking reasons for the continuance of that belief, and by acting to bring that belief into practical reality. This is the role of dynamic universalism which involves striving for a dynamic view of the universe and our place in it.

To be a dynamic universalist is to live a straightforward, wholesome life naked before the universe. Everything that the dynamic universalist does is laid before the universe and is not to be hidden in dark corners. This is because all our deeds, and the things that happen to us, even when they occur in private, are nevertheless potentially knowable. They are etched on the fabric of the universe at the very moment that they occur.

Therefore, they will be knowable in the future by intelligent beings who possess the technology required to access such knowledge. It is in the interests of us all to be dynamic universalists for the following reasons:

1. We enrich our lives when we relate to society by using the universalist outlook to open our minds to life's possibilities. Those who are already in tune with the society in which they live, have already adopted a universalist outlook without knowing it by that name. They may for instance call it 'humanism', plain 'optimism', or whatever.

2. Dynamic universalism helps us to think of our lives in terms of how it will seem to posterity. It enables us to broaden our minds so that we think more easily and happily beyond the present time. This means that we are not content to live in the present alone but are eager and willing to look to the future. But this often requires a distinctive change of mind, or *metanoia,* to broaden our outlook in this way.

There is no escaping a universalist belief of some kind. It is built into the very structure of our language. For everyone is a universalist by virtue of their ability to use universal terms such as 'the human race', 'the universe', 'the future', and so on. Suppose someone says: "I don't believe in universalism and I am not a universalist." In saying these words meaningfully, the person must understand the meaning of concepts such as 'universalism' and 'universalist', otherwise they are gibbering. These concepts can only be understood in relation to universal terms such as 'the human race', 'life', 'the universe' etc. If these terms have a meaning for a person then they must believe in the existence or non-existence of what they refer to. They must therefore believe at least in the possibility of something existing apart from themselves in the external world. And as they can only use universal terms to refer to these things, they are themselves universalists not matter how strenuously they attempt to deny the fact. In fact, the more they strive to deny their belief, the more evidence they are providing of that very belief, since they must use more and more universal terms to bolster their argument.

This applies, for example, to Nietzsche who, for all his nihilism, believed in the possibility of the *Übermensch* in the future as being a good and positive thing which could evolve out of humankind for all its flaws. He also referred to 'higher culture' not only in a positive way but also as something secure and perennial notwithstanding its being 'misunderstood' and misused at present.[7] Thus, even he could not avoid adopting a universalist viewpoint when considering the future possibilities of the human race.

Self-Accounting. In adopting the universalist view, it is helpful to give a good account of ourselves. Such an account is essential to our self-esteem. As we cannot be said to know ourselves unless we are clear about what we are and what we are aiming to do in life. In place of prayer and confession, this comprises a form of self-exhortation and self-clarification that puts us at one with ourselves and our place in the universe.

We give a good account of ourselves: (a) by getting clear about what we are as a person - our strengths and weaknesses; (b) by rising above the sordid details of everyday life to gain a unified view of ourselves; (c) by completing ourselves by tackling perceived weaknesses so as to build up our willpower and strength of character; (d) by learning to act in accordance with our idea of ourselves and thereby behave ourselves; (e) by understanding ourselves in relation to the universe as a whole; and (f) by looking forward to the future becoming better than the present and acting accordingly. Thus, we achieve greater self-knowledge.

Whatever a person says, thinks or does is important and significant in itself as long as it reflects their whole personality and is in concord with social norms and the universe as a whole. For such universalist activities comprise the individual's unique contribution to the content of the universe. Failing to do those things which are worthy of a person means that the universe is deprived of their benefit and is therefore the worse for their omission. This responsibility for the universe flows naturally from our being an intimate part and product of the universe.

The human self is discontinuous and fragmentary, and is liable to fall apart completely unless it is constantly bolstered and reinforced by positive thinking and by restrained and purposeful behaviour. To counter this desultory tendency, we must constantly strive to bring ourselves together in terms of our aims and goals in life. We achieve this by introspection to monitor our behaviour and organise ourselves in a positive and disciplined way. We thereby build up our inner life and become more integrated and purposeful in thought and behaviour. This is of course the aim of *vivoplenia* as outlined in part three above.

Many of the diseases of the modern world result from the failure to maintain this constant activity of self unification. Cancer, multiple sclerosis, anorexia, bulimia etc. result at least in part from a deficiency of inner self activity. According to this view, the person suffering from these diseases loses touch with themselves in a fundamental way. To avoid such symptoms of inner dissolution, we need to unify ourselves in terms of the whole self, its aims and goals. And we begin to do this by making a rational account of ourselves, by putting into words what we are and what we aim to do with our lives. Such self-knowledge makes us more sensitive to our inner workings and therefore more co-ordinated in mind and body. We think of ourselves as whole instead of as a succession of random thoughts and feelings.

Getting ourselves together as a whole is also a step towards attaining a state of wisdom. Being wise consists in doing the best possible things for the best possible reasons. But knowing what is best means taking the largest possible view of things at the time that we make a decision. We then take into account the greatest possible range of factors that we are capable of comprehending at any moment in time. This can only be done effectively when we are in touch with ourselves and all our past experiences and skills so that we marshal ourselves appropriately to meet the demands of the occasion and cope with them effectively. There is more on the importance of wisdom in my book, *Sagacity: The Way to Wisdom* (2019).

Understanding the Universe. A necessary precursor to getting in tune with the universe is acquiring an understanding of its workings and of our place in it. A thorough knowledge of the universe can be acquired through the study of astronomy, astrophysics and the sciences in general. If the education system fails to educate the individual in such matters, then it has failed in its duty to humanity and to life. Indeed, a good educational background is a necessary precursor to getting anything done in society. The better educated that we are, the more we are able to navigate our way confidently through the stormy seas of modern society.

Ten Steps towards the Universalist View. There are ten steps to getting in tune with the universe. They lead us to a particular universal view called 'dynamic' because it is not a static theory but a constant doing and thinking about things. These steps are specifically directed at the male gender since men are particularly in need of self-improvement and these provide a way of doing so:

(i) *Accepting that there is more to life than a purely humdrum materialist outlook.*

A totally materialist person can never aspire to the universalist outlook as long as he can see nothing beyond the material bodies available to the senses. Unless he can elevate his mind to an abstract level beyond that of the purely material, he will not see the problems and possibilities lying before the human race at that level of thought. While the mind is totally material, yet its subjectivity gives it imaginative powers that take it beyond the commonplace to see things as a whole.

(ii) *Undertaking to improve our minds and behaviour for purposes greater than ourselves*

Anyone who lives entirely for himself and is totally content with a lazy and aimless lifestyle, lacks the frame of mind to become a universalist. For being a universalist means having an intimate concern about what is happening in the world, even though we may have no opportunity to do anything about world events.

(iii) *Achieving the metanoia or change of mind which is necessary for the mind to be receptive to universal concepts and ideas.*

Becoming a universalist means proceeding towards the goal of *metanoia* or change of mind. This *metanoia* is achieved when the individual's mind is completely open to the universe so that it can be in tune with its rhythms and movements. This is not a religious or psychological state of mind but a PHILOSOPHICAL one. The mind is being trained in a particular way to handle ideas about ourselves and the universe.

(iv) *Thinking about our own place in the universe and in relation to the human race at large.*

Everyone is faced with making their own effort to come to terms with the universe and their place in it. It is an important part of being an adult in a sophisticated modern society. But there is nothing more mystical and unfathomable than our link with the universe as a whole. Science is only slowly approaching a complete understanding of this link. There is still much that is mystifying even to the most knowledgeable of scientists. Universalists are concerned about making sense of this link because the act of doing so helps to keep them in tune with the universe.

(v) *Completing ourselves as a person who has a clear role to play in the universe.*

The ability to think of ourselves in relation to the universe as a whole helps us to approach the goal of completing ourselves so that we can think of ourselves as a whole. We are no longer a series of unconnected experiences. We can then relate everything that happens to our overall conception of ourselves.

(vi) *Giving a good account of ourselves in relation to the universe as a whole.*

Having an overall conception of ourselves as a whole, is a necessary prerequisite to being able to give a good account of ourselves. This means justifying our beliefs, opinions, and actions in relation to that overall conception. It is getting ourselves together as mature persons with a coherent view of the world and our place in the universe.

(vii) *Acquiring knowledge about the universe and everything in it including life, the human race and its culture.*

Being a mature and self-motivated human being means increasing our understanding of the universe from a scientific point of view. Scientific knowledge is indispensible to the universalist point of view. Knowledge is power and the more knowledge we acquire the more we gain mastery of ourselves and our links with the universe as a whole. The key to understanding ourselves thus lies ultimately in scientific progress in understanding what the universe is all about.

(viii) *Helping to make things better for life on earth by co-operating with others within the social limits imposed on us.*

The next stage is to realise how little we can accomplish as solitary individuals. If we are to contribute to the future well-being of the human race and life in general, even in a very small way, we must co-operate with others to achieve common aims. It is however necessary to do this only within rational and legal limits. And these limits are inevitably laid down by the society we find ourselves. We can only be at one with each other by operating within the sphere of society.

(ix) *Finding our place in society so that we can acquiesce in such grand plans as, for instance, the spreading of life throughout the universe.*

Finding our place in society involves personal confrontation with the universal principles laid down here so that we use them to make the best possible use of our lives. This means incorporating these principles into our everyday thinking about things. They become part of the way we think and feel about everything that is happening around us.

(x) *Becoming a wholehearted Universalist in thought, word and deed.*

The ability to conform to universal principles so that we have complete self-command, is what distinguishes the fully-fledged universalist. For the true universalist has no problem relating personal and emotional needs and aims with overriding universalist objectives. The dynamic nature of his thinking ensures that his attitudes and opinions are always adjusting and evolving to make sense of the situation in which he finds himself. Being a wholehearted universalist is more than holding any particular faith, dogma or specific set of beliefs. Universalism puts all our beliefs into the widest possible context so that we can see them from afar and put them in their true place in the scheme of things. It is an attitude of mind in which we are optimistic concerning the prospects facing humanity. It is also a determination to maintain a purity of thought and deed no matter what the corrupting influences of an immoral world may throw at us.

The Universalist Viewpoint is Important. Dynamic universalism offers an overall view that helps to unify all human activities. The 'invisible hand'[8] of selfish human activity is not enough to ensure the cohesion of human society as opposed to its ever-present threat to descend into enmity, war, anarchy and chaos. Thus, it is highly desirable for society to have the conscious and rational participation of every individual in willingly contributing to the greater whole to avoid the kind of alienation, conflict, and division that causes the disintegration of social ties and bonds. In Adam Smith's system, the notion of 'sympathy' between all human beings provided the necessary underlying social cohesive factor.[9] In other 18th century philosophies, notions such as benevolence (Hutcheson)[10] and goodwill (Kant)[11] played a similar part.

Universalism casts light on the puzzle of how philosophical inquiry in the clubs and societies of the Scottish Enlightenment led their members to be concerned about practical, everyday matters, as well as abstract problems of science, philosophy and religion. They worried a lot about the local economy, the manufacturing industry, agriculture, fisheries, and the plight of labourers and the poor, just as much as about the biology of plants, the perception of external objects, and the existence of the deity. This is because they expanded their thinking in universal terms to include their concerns about society and the human race as a whole. In thus identifying themselves with the plight of the whole human race, they became more compassionate and concerned about the welfare of everyone. They were not concerned with abstract notions in a non-universalist manner, i.e. in a Platonic manner. For that divorces these notions from their human context. Unlike universalism, which leads us back into concrete, down-to-earth concerns, Platonism takes us to the stratosphere where we drift aimlessly into outer space. For the latter treats such notions as entities in their own right, over and above their connections with human beings who alone can give them existence by using them appropriately. Once they are severed from their common sense connections then they can proceed endlessly to infinity and give rise to the endless and fruitless speculations of conspiracy theorists and the like.

The Interactivity of Notional Usage. Universal notions such as good, truth, beauty, love, justice, and honour are interactive in their usage. The universalist view ensures that they are not treated like the eternal, changeless things envisaged by Plato. We use them interactively in seeking knowledge about the world, about other people and, most importantly, about ourselves and what we really feel about things. Socrates famously never arrived at satisfactory definitions of words such as justice, piety and knowledge. This is because of their interactivity. We use them interrogatively and ask: Is this view true or not? Do I love this person or not? Is this just or not? In questioning things in that way we are interacting with them. They are the source of the value we put on things, and there is more on the evaluative nature of universal notions in my book, *The Way of Togetherness* (2019) in section 7, pp. 122-144.

Why do we have the ability to form and use these universal notions? In the view of dynamic universalism, the most important answer is: so that we may use them to justify our place in the universe. We know this because these notions can be used to point to the future. We can use them to imagine what our place in the universe may or may not be. And we can imagine ourselves having a better place in the universe than we have at present, even though that role may still be infinitesimally small in relation to the universe as a whole. Nevertheless, the fact that we possess such imaginative powers means that we have the capacity to justify our place in the universe in our imaginings. Also, when we think of these universal notions in practical terms, this can only be because we have them in mind to use them in some future circumstances. We use them to lend meaning and purpose to our actions by relating the latter to universal concerns such as those of life and the human race. This ability to form and use universal notions therefore gives rise to the primary purpose of universalism which is to take humanity forward and achieve real and meaningful progress.

We are important to the universe in that we are at the cutting edge of it; we are the scythe by which universe cuts its way through to the future. Nothing else can achieve this. In a sense, each of us *is* the universe as far as we are concerned. When we are born, our universe comes into existence; when we die, that universe dies with us, though what we have contributed during our lifetimes never dies. What has happened in the past can never be destroyed, and the events of our lives remain out there always to be accessed. Therefore, our existence is necessary to that universe since it cannot exist without us. Doubtless, other universes continue to exist for other people after we die but as far as each of us concerned, we are the universe.

The purpose of our existence is to bring greater order to the universe than what existed before. We do this in our daily lives by behaving sensibly, by making sense of our situation and by putting things in a better order than before. By simply being content with ourselves as we are, we are in a sense creating order by ensuring that things continue as they are and do not degrade or fall apart. The universe is all the better for our existence when we make more of it by doing and being ourselves.

We may consider ourselves god-like in creating the universe for ourselves as we imbibe more and more information about it. But we must also humble ourselves by realising the extent of our ignorance and of our smallness in relation to the unimaginable vastness of the universe. All we can do is accumulate ever greater experiences in our living within it and make the best of that personal knowledge for the benefit of life and humanity as a whole.

Each of us is alone within that universe unless we reach out to invite others into our universe or are invited into theirs in turn. This is the purpose of social unity; it brings us altogether to broaden and deepen our respective universes so that we make ourselves as inclusive as humanly possible. We remain locked in a lonely universe of our own making, unless we reach out and embrace the universe as a whole. Thus, the universalist view gives us the tools to develop inwardly so that we can incorporate in a holist way that which is outside us. In that way, we become ourselves more completely and become more content and happier within our skins.

The Prospectivist View

Life-belief also means ensuring that life prospers in the future. This prospective view is lacking in religion in so far as it is enslaved by its past. The prospectivist view looks to the future and uses the past to build a better future. The word 'prospective' comes from the Latin 'prospectus' which is the past participle of 'prospicere' – 'to look forward' or 'to look into the distance'.[12] The prospective view is relatively new since it is more natural for us to live in the past and not think too much of the future since it is fraught with uncertainties.

It was evolution and science fiction in the 19th century that led people to look to the future with any optimism, and H.G. Wells was in the vanguard of that. He was the first to make clear the distinction between 'prospective' and 'retrospective'. Looking to the future is a *prospective* viewpoint, and looking to the past is a *retrospective* viewpoint. He made this distinction (though not in these words) in a lecture in the Royal Institution in 1902, subsequently published as *The Discovery of the Future.* He distinguished two attitudes of mind: the backward-looking 'legal mind', and the forward-looking 'creative mind'.[13] Many people have the first attitude of mind and scarcely think of the future at all. Wells thought that the more 'modern' view is the latter which "is constructive in habit, it interprets the things of the present and gives value to this and that, entirely in relation to the things designed or foreseen." However, he acknowledged that "the great mass of people occupy an intermediate position between these extremes."[14]

It helps us all to believe that life and humanity have a future on this planet and in this universe. Our lives make more sense when we think of them as contributing to a better future. By looking to the future in a positive way, we can see that things can be better in the future if we work hard enough to ensure that they are better, even though current events may make that future look bleak and forbidding. We need to look at the past as teaching us how to make things better in the future.

The prospective view therefore does not supersede the retrospective view. It provides the context in which the past can be used for the benefit of the future. The retrospective view therefore contributes to the prospective one to ensure that we learn the lessons of the past instead of being dominated by the past, as is the case with many religions – Roman Catholicism, Buddhism etc.

Though we never know exactly what that future holds for us, we can do much in the present to ensure, not only that we do have a future, but also that we make the future better for posterity, that is, for future generations. By adopting the prospective point of view, we concentrate more intently on the practical difficulties of making the future better. We are naturally critical of whatever is happening in the present that is not conducive to the welfare of posterity. The avoidance of wars and unnecessary conflict are examples of futile and self-destructive behaviour that contributes nothing positive to posterity. We need both prospectivism and retrospectivism as long as they are not taken to extremes as they need to remain in close relationship to each other when we try to make the best of the future before us.

The extremes of retrospectivism. Extreme retrospectivists include those monks and nuns who live cloistered in the past, also those rock'n'rollers who live rooted in the sixties and seventies, and anyone who would rather live in the past or in some legendary Golden Age. In contrast, prospectivists appreciate the past only as a gateway to the future. We learn from the past, but don't dwell in it.

Extreme retrospectivism is monistic in outlook in so far as the past is experienced as one unchanging thing. The writer of *Ecclesiastes* in the *Old Testament* was a retrospectivist for whom "there is nothing new under the sun". Considering all the novel accomplishments of modern civilisation, it seems absurd to argue that nothing new is being created that did not exist before. For example, it is a completely new thing to write book like this on a computer without using a pen or a typewriter.

When organisations such as the Roman Catholic Church resist changes, they are usually being retrospective in their view. They tend to recreate the past in the present without thinking of the future as being any different, let alone better. The prospectivist thinks about how future generations would benefit from knowing about Catholicism - its merits as well as its faults.

The extremes of retrospectivism. An extreme prospective view consists in our leaving everything be sorted out in the future. It leads us to do nothing for ourselves in the present. It tells us to let posterity take care of all our present problems. The extreme prospectivist also believes in the inevitability of human progress which will occur whatever we do in the present. The French philosopher Auguste Comte adopted such an extreme prospective view in his positivism that saw progress as being inevitable, while at the same time adopting an extreme retrospectivist view in respect of his religious doctrines which re-invented Catholicism in the guise of humanism.[15]

There are obvious limits to the prospective view in that we cannot live from day to day worrying about what may not happen. During the Cold War period, when a nuclear Armageddon was a distinct possibility, most people went about their daily business hardly giving it a thought. And they were proved right to do so, since nothing came of these remote fears. Even during the Cuban missile crisis of 1962, when there was a real threat of nuclear war, there was no panic in the streets as most people didn't want to believe that war was impending. Nowadays, there may be even more chance of a nuclear attack than there was then, as wars are still plaguing us, and there are malignant terrorists around who might perpetrate such an act if they could. But once again people don't want to dwell too much on such possibilities.

Relating the prospective and retrospective views. Generally speaking, the prospective view is optimistic about the future and the retrospective view is pessimistic about the future. We often oscillate between these points of view when we are uncertain about our future. For a balanced point of view, we need both of these outlooks so that the one is balanced in relation to the other in an interactive way. However, the prospective view must predominate over the retrospective view to ensure continued progress into the future.

In the past, the human race was overwhelmingly retrospectivist in its outlook. It is not natural for us to look too much to the future, so retrospectivism is the default position to which we all revert unless we consciously adopt a prospective view. We are all retrospectivists to some extent when we immerse ourselves in the past and make too much of it. But if we want to make the most of our lives, we need to be prospective and use our retrospective tendencies to balance them with our prospective ones. After WW2 we became more accustomed to looking forward to the future with pleasure and anticipation instead of fear and apprehension. However, pessimism has grown more recently about our future due to the nationalistic slide towards WW3 and the lack of a philosophical consensus to halt that decline. Pessimism about the future makes people more prone to the retrospective outlook.

Studying history helps us to avoid repeating the mistakes of the past. We learn from history but we need not dwell on it. We is not beneficial for us to relive the past as if it were *ipso facto* better than the present. We can enjoyably relive past lives such that of Samuel Pepys in his diary and in so doing we learn how things were different in the past though the same in some ways but no better overall. People's lives in the past could be just as full and complex as our lives but in different ways.

We can keep posterity in perspective while being retrospectivists who value the contribution of the past, but only to the extent that it can be used for future benefit. As prospectivists, we believe in the possibility of posterity rather than its actuality. We are unsure whether there will be a future posterity. The very doubtfulness of its future existence is a spur to us to do our utmost to ensure that it comes into being in the future. It all depends on us and what we do now. We must also recognise that on the one hand posterity could be much greater than we can possibly think or on onthe other hand it may not come to anything at all. It can go either way or none at all. The very uncertainty is necessary to ensure that we are not complacent about the future. Thus, being overly sure about such future prospects is an extreme form of prospectivism that makes too much of the future.

Applying the Prospective View. The prospective view aims to bring the past to the attention of future generations. In that way, prospectivism includes all humanity's achievements including religion. Prospectivists think about these things in relation to their future reception rather than simply recreating the past. They look forward to better things rather than looking to the past as always being preferable to the present or the future. Thus, in this view, the study of religion becomes more a matter of contemplation than of rigid adherence and unquestioned devotion. The more thoughtful that a religion becomes, the more it appreciates life-belief and the idea of a better future. An unthoughtful religion is obsessed entirely with its own beliefs and rejects anything that renders these beliefs doubtful.

Prospectivism is one of the best belief systems available to humanity as long as it remains self-critical and scientific in its aspirations. It epitomises the vivodoxian attempt to embrace all other belief systems, since it contributes to the conceptual framework within which they may all be studied, contemplated and put in their rightful place in the overall canon of human thought. Prospectivism is concerned for the future of humanity in three senses: (1) it points to the future; (2) it reflects a future that embraces all religions; (3) it gives the human race a future to look forward to.

Prospectivism is not itself a religious endeavour. It is a scientific and rational belief system that makes sense of religion in so far we can make sense of it. Relating religion to our future prospects is one way in which prospectivism makes sense of it. The more that a religion is related to future prospects, the more sensible it is. Prospectivism is scientific in being falsifiable and the subject of constant doubt. We can never say that it is true since we are constantly doubtful whether the human race will make it in the future. As already pointed out, that very doubt encourages us to do our utmost to ensure its future. Also, we can evaluate our present activities in terms of what they may mean to future generations. This makes possible a system of evaluation by which prospective judgments are made concerning the future consequences of our actions.

Having the courage to believe in our future is necessary to ensure that we do have a future. People nowadays are even less rosy and optimistic about our future prospects than in the days of H.G. Wells. There was then a universal optimism about the future that was lost after the WW1 and has never really been regained.[16] We are now much more aware of the threats to our future both internal and external. Clearly, we need to work very hard to ensure our place in the future, in view of our environmental destructiveness and the endless possibility of catastrophes, such as pandemics, comets, volcanoes, wars, and nuclear explosions, spoiling our promising future. Nevertheless, we have to believe in the future prospects of the human race before its prospects can be realised.

The good of civilisation requires that we look as much to the future as to the past. We must think about what will be better in the future and what will benefit future generations. The study of the future ought now to be pursued just as rigorously as the study of the past. And the latter study ought to be in the service of the former one. Our greatness as a species lies in what we make of the opportunities before us now. It does not lie in our feeble and uncoordinated actions in the past. It consists in what is to come and in our present efforts to ensure that things are better in the future. Everything that happened in the past has been, as H.G. Wells said, "but the twilight before the dawn" and past accomplishments have been "but the dream before the awakening." Our future thus consists in looking to the future, and prospective view tries to work out that viewpoint as consistently as possible. Wells summed up our future prospects as follows:

> We are creatures of the twilight. But it is out of our race and lineage that minds will spring, that will reach back to us in our littleness to know us better than we know ourselves, and that will reach forward fearlessly to comprehend this future that defeats our eyes.[17]

Our perennial task is to ensure that the human race continues into the future despite all the threats to that future. This can best be achieved by unifying humanity and eliminating the divisions of race, religion, nationality that set us against each other for no good reason. The unity of the human race must be emphasised and in that respect, Vivodoxia or life-belief can save us from ourselves by stressing our unity.

How not to advance humanity. We will not be better human beings by altering ourselves in arbitrary ways by means of genetic engineering or brain implants; least of all by converting ourselves into machine-like cyborgs or allowing super-intelligent robots to enslave us. Above all, we must never lose our humanity. It is worth noting that the androids and holograms in the Star Trek television series are always striving to be more human and they regret being less than human. For example, being human consists in being subject to unpredictable intuitions, which give rise to our creativity and ingenuity. As argued previously, such intuitive powers seem to have deep biological roots and perhaps result from quantum activity that will not be readily accessible to proponents of artificial intelligence.

The use of artificial intelligence to achieve so-called 'transhumanism' is not a viable means of advancing humanity if it threatens to our future as a species. We will not be any better for becoming machines, and the creation of intelligent robots may lead to the extinction of the human race as many people have warned.[18] Artificial means of replacing missing limbs and organs and remedying other bodily defects are admissible and commendable. Equally laudable are attempts to prolong our lives and perhaps conquer death altogether. But using anything else to give one person artificial advantage over the rest of us is comparable to using drugs to enhance athletic performance. We don't need to create new types of human being when we are already an immensely diverse species.

It is therefore arguable that we would not advance ourselves by cybernetic means, such as inserting computer chips into brains, or adding devices to make us function more like machines than human beings. If enhanced individuals have mathematical or other skills that are beyond the normal human range of ability then they set themselves apart from the rest of us, like the X-men of the feature film series. This possibility is made worse by advocates of transhumanism which aims to "greatly enhance longevity, cognition, and well-being", according to the Wikipedia article on the subject. Transhumanism propounds the following laws:

1. A transhumanist must safeguard one's own existence above all else.

2. A transhumanist must strive to achieve omnipotence as expediently as possible – as long as one's actions do not conflict with the First Law.

3. A transhumanist must safeguard value in the universe – as long as one's actions do not conflict with the First and Second Laws.[19]

These laws are extraordinarily egotistic. The First Law could sanction the killing of human beings who disapprove of transhumanism on the grounds that their opinions threaten the transhumanist's existence. Perhaps these laws should be preceded by Asimov's Robotic Laws:

1. A robot may not injure a human being or, through inaction, allow a human being to come to harm.

2. A robot must obey the orders given it by human beings except where such orders would conflict with the First Law.

3. A robot must protect its own existence as long as such protection does not conflict with the First or Second Laws.[20]

The whole transhumanist enterprise is fraught with difficulties because it puts newfangled beings above and beyond us. We can never be happy with superior beings lording themselves over us, especially if they are of our own making. Intelligent robots cannot be allowed to take over and their activities would be very strictly limited and subject of human control and monitoring.

It may be that that a so-called 'singularity' will be reached in which computers become a life form of their own. If this is the case, we could perhaps eliminate any threat to us by sending such life forms into outer space on long missions to far-off planets, solar systems and galaxies. They would be free of the biological constraints that presently confine us to the surface of this planet. They could be put on space vehicles containing seeds and frozen embryos that could spread life throughout the universe. This is the modern relevance of the biblical Noah's Ark story.

In the meantime, we ourselves are slowly adapting to living in outer space by means of the experiments being conducted on the International Space Station.   Thus, human beings may eventually be capable of thriving in outer space by making the physiological adaptations necessary to do so. Any further advances could take place in outer space and leave the rest of us in peace. Indeed, anything that becomes uncomfortably more advanced than we are, can be dealt with by sending such advanced beings *en masse* where no mere human beings dare to go and thus conquer outer space for the benefit of us all.

The Unifying View

Vivodoxia or life-belief can also be used as a focal point of unity by which the world is unified for the future benefit of humanity. It offers a common philosophy that brings us together as a species. As a symbol of unity, it points to the future and that was basically the message of the Jesuit priest, Teilhard de Chardin. In books such as *The Phenomenon of Man,* he argued for a final unity called 'Omega Point'.[21] For there is a tendency for material things to go beyond themselves and produce more complex, unified beings. This process has led to increasingly complex entities from quantum particles through to atoms, molecules, cells, and organisms. Finally, complex living beings have culminated in the human body which has evolved with a sophisticated nervous system that permits rational reflection, self-awareness, and moral responsibility. He pointed out that the appearance of man has brought an added dimension into the world. This is the birth of reflection: animals know, but man *knows* that he knows; he has knowledge to the square, as he seems to have thought.

Teilhard also valued the evolution of human society which he interpreted as the 'noosphere' – the mind sphere – which has emerged above the biosphere of living beings since the advent of humanity. There has been in recent centuries a cultural convergence towards a single society – a 'global village'[22] brought together by improved communications and travelling opportunities. He saw evolution as a progression towards convergence – "an organo-psychic convergence of the world upon itself"[23] that contrasts with the physical expansion of the universe. However, he interpreted this convergence in a religious way as a unifying point identified as God and therefore as the divine Christ leading towards this convergence. The *Encyclopaedia Britannica* article about him puts it this way:

> "Theologically, Teilhard saw the process of organic evolution as a sequence of progressive syntheses whose ultimate convergence point is that of God. When humanity and the material world have reached their final state of evolution and exhausted all potential for further development, a new convergence between them and the supernatural order would be initiated by the Parousia, or Second Coming of Christ."[24]

The prospective view follows this kind of Teilhardian view but not its theological implications. It looks forward to a better future without harking back to time-worn Christian doctrines that divinise Jesus instead of treating him as the common man to whom we can all relate as human beings. Teilhard was more concerned with reconciling his views to orthodox Christian doctrines than with reconciling the views of Jesus of Nazareth to current knowledge. In my book *Jesus of Nazareth: The Real Man and his Message* (2019) I examine the evidence for Jesus being a real person living in the first century CE. He was all too human in his rash behaviour in the temple that was his downfall, and the extreme guilt of his followers at leaving him to his fate led to the beliefs to which Christians adhere to this day. In that book, I discuss all this, together with a contemporary treatment of his message.

The Unifying Role of Love. In a way, love is the prime unifying force in the universe. This is love in the sense of things coming together to interact harmoniously. It is love as an interaction that creates unities which persist into the future but not indefinitely. Life and humanity constitute the acme of complex loving relationships but only when they look to the future and attempt to contribute to that future, one way or another. Loving relationships that are confined to the present or rooted in the past are selfish and self-centred. Love has no real meaning unless it contributes to unity and harmony and the future of humanity, as in the case of reproduction or creative activity of some kind.

The prospective view looks forward to the increasing unity and orderliness that both life and humanity bring into the universe. This unity and orderliness trends towards a *cosmic unity* that has emerged from the natural processes of the universe. It is greatly accelerated by the growing purposefulness of living beings. This is not God but a purposeful trend in the material universe leading to the potential unity of the universe in the far future.

The Unifying Forces of the Universe. Entities come together naturally by the four forces of physics, namely, the strong and weak atomic forces, and the electro-magnetic and gravitational forces. Each entity comprises a unified pocket of orderliness and harmony during its existence. Life and humanity themselves result from these unifying processes of the universe, as is described in astronomy, physics, biology and the other sciences (albeit as yet incompletely). The ubiquity of this unifying activity throughout the universe is therefore confirmed by scientific research. In these respects, prospective view of life-belief is wholly compatible with what science tells us about the universe. We are all products of universal processes that are trending towards this cosmic unity and we all can make our individual contributions to that trend.

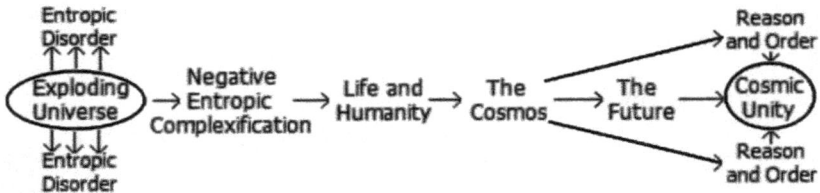

Entropic Disorder ↑↑↑ → (Exploding Universe) → Negative Entropic Complexification → Life and Humanity → The Cosmos → The Future → (Cosmic Unity) → Reason and Order ↘; with Reason and Order ↗ above; Entropic Disorder ↓↓↓ below Exploding Universe.

This rough diagram shows the universe exploding into 'entropic disorder' which is happening all around us. Though everything in the universe falls apart eventually, there is an accumulation of complexity that is passed on. This complexifying strand of 'negative entropy' goes against the entropic trend. As stars explode, they pass on their accumulated complexities which form part of successive stars, each contributing their respective complexifications in the form of heavier elements such as carbon that forms the basis of life. Likewise, life contributes to this growth in complexity, as we do as individuals when we add to humanity's accumulated experiences.

When life emerged out of the natural complexifying processes of the universe, more complex life-forms became possible, and humanity as a whole is the most complex of all life-forms so far. Humanity's complex social activity has given rise to 'The Cosmos' which, in this context, incorporates all our reasonable and orderly activity in which we are creating and making things. After that 'The Future' can lead toward greater 'Cosmic Unity' by means of 'Reason and Order' which life, and especially intelligent beings, can bring into the universe. By 'reason' is meant not only logical reasoning but all our inductive and intuitive reasonings. This includes not only the progress of scientific knowledge and understanding but also art, literature, engineering and every activity that can be put into meaningful words, symbols, images and physical objects. This all consists of ordering of one sort or another. The cosmic unity therefore reflects the possibilities lying before us, assuming we are up to the task.

The cosmic growth in complexity that has resulted in our complex human culture is summed up in the following approximate progression:

> energy → elementary particles → atoms → heavy elements → molecules → amino acids → single cells → multi-cellular organisms → animals and plants → mammals → human beings → human culture → cosmos → cosmic unity

Energy coalesces into elementary particles, which then come together to form atoms. The constant addition of protons, neurons and electrons to the atomic structure produces progressively heavier and more complex elements. These elements come together to form molecules that culminate in complex amino acids which come together to make DNA possible. The complexity of single cells is compounded by their coming together to form complex organisms that are divided into the two families of active animals and passive plants. The complex social structures of mammals have led to human beings, the most cultured, devious and deadly of all animals. The complexity of human culture surpasses that of all other living beings on the planet, and this contributes to the cosmos but only when human activities are reasonable, orderly and positively creative. The unifying activity of the cosmos points ultimately to cosmic unity at the end of things. Thus, all that we are doing in the present makes more sense from this higher perspective. Contemplating that perspective motivates us to do our best and overcome our shortcomings.

Starting from energy, each of the entities in the above progression has an internal structure which is progressively more complex than the ones coming before. The physical forces mentioned above have brought into existence the earliest entities as unified structures. But even the most complex entities only preserve their unity for a limited period of time, during which they are centres of order and harmony. At each stage in the complexification process, the entities acquire more powers to establish order and harmony within themselves. These powers result from increasing interactions between the parts comprising them, and the powers are used when living beings act purposefully in feeding and reproducing themselves and in combating other entities such as viruses and bacteria that threaten their existence.

Though death and dissolution are ubiquitous and unavoidable, whatever is left behind is not lost as it is available to whatever incorporates the contents of the defunct entity. Nothing lasts forever but while it does last, it accumulates unique attributes that enrich the whole after death or dissolution. This is as true of stars as it is of living beings.

But the complexity of living beings means that they have more to contribute to their successors after their dissolution. Thus, death has no sting since it contributes to the accumulative trend towards ultimate togetherness that is possible in the future and will be witnessed by posterity, as long as we do our best to ensure its future existence.

Moreover, our very sociability contributes to cosmic unity. The more we do for each other, the better we can live together and work together to achieve great and worthwhile things. Thus, the role of service is important in the prospective view of things. We serve each other and society at large. In so doing we add meaning and purpose to our lives and those of others. Our love and affection for each other is itself a great unifying factor. Such feelings bring us together in our common interests and activities. All this contributes to the Teilhardian convergence of society towards increasing unity.

As argued above on page 43, our existence is necessary to the universe since it cannot exist without us. It requires observers such as ourselves to perceive it and to form theories about it, and in that sense it does not exist without us. This view heralds the importance of life and humanity in contributing more to the universe than what existed before. Though we are physically infinitesimally small in that universe, we are nevertheless immeasurably large in our effects on things at the other end of the scale. We are in a medial position between the very large and the very small, and this makes us immensely important in what we can do to take life forward into the future. There is more on the centrality of our position in the universe in my book, *The Way of Togetherness*, pp. 173-186.

> We look forward to the time when the Power of Love will replace the Love of Power. Then will our world know the blessings of peace.
>
> William E. Gladstone

This quotation is also attributed to Dr. William Ellery Channing (1780-1842) and less convincingly to Jimi Hendrix.

Part Five

Bringing Religions Together

The Abiding Need for Religion

As early as 1902, William James wrote: "There is a notion in the air about us that religion is probably only an anachronism, a case of 'survival', an atavistic relapse into a mode of thought which humanity in its more enlightened examples has outgrown."[25] He was right to disagree with this. Events during the twentieth century have shown him to be correct. Last century saw a succession of failures to downgrade religion and replace it, especially in communist countries where a complete ban has not worked; a resurgence of religion occurred in most of these countries towards the end of the century. Humanism as a creed has also failed to replace people's need for religious faith. For example, the philosopher Bertrand Russell tried very hard to disparage religion in works such as *Why I am not a Christian* (1957) where he says:

> Religion prevents our children from having a rational education; religion prevents us from removing the fundamental causes of war; religion prevents us from removing teaching the ethic of scientific co-operation in place of the old fierce doctrines of sin and punishment. It is possible that mankind is on the threshold of a golden age; but, if so, it will be necessary first to slay the dragon that guards the door, and this dragon is religion.[26]

Even if it were possible "to slay the dragon", it is not certain that a golden age would be ushered in. People's need for religion is too strong, and religion can reform itself to give a better education, be more receptive of the scientific view, become less warlike, and more ethical. Life-belief can be used to make religion more relevant to the future of humanity, and less dependent on its more inhumane and objectionable past.

William James's book, *The Varieties of Religious Experience* is a psychological study of people's personal need for religion. He argues that religion fulfils the need for transcendence beyond the everyday world. But philosophy itself can fulfil that need. At its best, religion is personal to everyone and makes sense of their lives for them. At its worst, it stultifies their growth and development through excessive authoritarianism.

It takes all sorts to make a world. All the different attitudes of mind combine to give us the diverse human culture in which we live. Or in James's more convoluted language: "Each attitude being a syllable in human nature's total message, it takes the whole of us to spell out the meaning completely".[27] The atheist's view is complemented by the theist's view. The atheist thinks that God is a figment of the imagination – a dream that people cling to without reason or evidence. In contrast, the god-believer sees God everywhere and cannot conceive of a world without such a being behind everything that exists. Even at such extremes, they have a belief in life in common. Even if they believe that life is not worth living, they can at least understand what such belief means, and can perhaps be persuaded to change their minds regarding the value of their own lives.

Our similarities are as important as our differences. As Dr. Johnson put it: "We are all prompted by the same motives, all deceived by the same fallacies, all animated by hope, obstructed by danger, entangled by desire, and seduced by pleasure."[28] If we are all the same in the perils and opportunities that we face in life, we have enough in common to appreciate the value of each other's lives, no matter how different we are in attitudes, opinions and beliefs.

The Role of Religions

All religions make their respective contributions to humanity. Studying these contributions is important as they all say something about the human condition and about what it is to be human. But this is only when we consider them historically. Much of their value is lost when they are made into active vehicles of absolute truth that are set against other religions. Their real significance depends on their no longer being proselytising religions whose truths are forced on people in an exclusive way that brooks no deviation from these truths. Priests, preachers, rabbis, mullahs and the like tell us that holy scriptures are bodies of truth coming from God, angels, aliens or wherever. We can better appreciate the value of scriptural content in its human context and not in any supernatural context. Thus, the big picture is inclusive of all religions even when their adherents apply them in an exclusive way. But crucially that inclusion is not uncritical but highly evaluative in seeing the true value in all religion.

Religious writings make their own contributions and this includes all sacred works of all the religions of the world, and most notably such texts as the Bible, the Talmud, the Koran, Buddhist scriptures, the Upanishads, and the Bhagavad Gita. The range of writings to be included can be seen in works such as A.C. Bouquet's *The Sacred Books of the World*.[29] This book includes writings as diverse as Sumerian Prayers, Homeric Hymns, Zoroastrian Literature, and Japanese Shinto Literature. We can add to this list our growing understanding of ancient religious writings such as those of the ancient Egyptians and Mayans. All these writings are important to our understanding of how human religious thought developed, and of how diverse that thought is. Although humanist thinking has transcended religious thought, the study of the latter helps us to understand the past trains of thought upon which we have advanced to our present state. This helps us to arrive at a better understanding of our plight and place in the universe.

Religious prophets are those people who have seen beyond the material world and have emphasised the importance of our musings about our existence. In a sense, we are all prophets who have our views of the nature of the universe and who strive to communicate these views to other people. Compared to the well-known prophets, most of us make fairly modest spiritual contributions to the overall view, such as this book here.

The most important of all the prophets who have walked the face of the Earth are those who have had the most impact on the history of the human race. They introduced new religions and thereby changed the thinking of humankind by these acts. The most important of all prophets include Akhenaton, Moses, Zoroaster, Buddha, Confucius, Jesus and Mohammed. Whether the effects of these prophets have been altogether to the good of humankind is entirely another matter. The overall view enables us to establish the real and lasting importance of these figures. We do so by accounting for their influence on their contemporaries, disciples, and followers. The facts about them can be studied objectively so that their true value to humanity can be established beyond doubt.

Religious beliefs contribute to humanity in so far as they add to our understanding of the human condition. We can study them within that context and not adhere to them as if they were eternal truths. We can learn from such studies. For instance, the distinctive advances of the Christian message contained in the Sermon of the Mount are permanent contributions to the cosmos, (see p. 32 above). We can all be *Christians* in our attitude towards our potential enemies and in our attempts to understand people rather than hate them. Equally, we can all be *Jews* in our respect for family life; *Muslims* in our respect for authority and absolute values; Buddhists in our use of meditation to reach our inner being; *Hindus* in our appreciation of spirituality; and so on. In this way, we can make use of the strengths of truths in particular religions without believing in the unbelievable, and without practising senseless, superfluous rituals like crouching down abjectly and to no purpose.

Such cosmic ideals were anticipated by the comparative religion movement which has its roots in the religious toleration established in Great Britain after the 17th century Civil War. In understanding the merits of religions in general, we can transcend them all within the context of the cosmos. Also, by taking account of all religions and respecting their respective contributions, we pass on to posterity what is worthwhile about them. It means liberating our thinking and our emotions to embrace all that humanity has to offer in the way of spirituality and self-belief.

The traditional religions clearly have no future as self-sufficient, mutually antagonistic movements. By themselves, they no longer take us anywhere as they have become too ingrown and limited in their outlook and lack competent answers to the human predicament. The exclusivity of these religions means that they exclude unbelievers and heretics. The four great prophets of religion – Moses, Jesus, Buddha, Confucius and Mohammed – give us great truths but not the whole truth. They got it wrong, each in their different ways. The first and last of these personages made far too much of a non-existent entity with the aim of belittling people unjustifiably and boosting their power over them without limit. Jesus made too much of unworldliness and meekness. The Buddha made too much of introspective meditation to the point of vacuity. Confucius made much of the value of older people but too much of our ancestry, They were all unable to see the bigger picture as they lacked access to the totality of humanity. Their view of human potential was also limited by the state of human knowledge available to them. Each succeeding generation needs to build on their achievements and not repeat their mistakes *ab nauseum* as the various religions are still doing to their everlasting shame.

Adhering to one religion to the exclusion of all others bolsters beliefs such as the following: that prophets were inspired by angels to write sacred texts, as believed by Mormons and Mohammedans; that extraterrestrials created or influenced the human race, as believed by Raelians and Scientologists; that people rise from the dead and be the 'Son of God', as believed by Christians; that people can reach a higher state of consciousness by spiritual exercises of one sort or another, as believed by Buddhists and New Ageists. Those who believe in such things in an exclusive way are treating such beliefs as inviolable truths. They disparage the disbelievers and have contempt for other faiths. We cannot move forward together while the various religions remain at loggerheads with each other and we lack common ends by which we can work together for a better future. Vivodoxia or life-belief offers such common ends in the spirit of accommodation and not confrontation.

Integrating Religions

We can embrace all religions in a coherent way. This possibility began with the Comparative Religion Movement of early to mid 20th century. This was a Christian based movement that attempted unsuccessfully to lay the foundations for a unified world religion. Until the 1970s, this unifying aim of comparative religion was generally believed to be the obvious way forward for all world religions. The following quotations taken from books on Islam and Hinduism show that this belief was widely accepted during the 20th century: The first is taken from a book by W. M. Watt called *Islamic Philosophy and Theology* and published in 1962:

> Each of the great religious communities is in closer contact with the other great religions than has ever been the case before. Members of the great religions are being forced, as never before, to

learn how to live alongside adherents of other faiths. Consequently, there are strong pressures urging men towards a unified world religion. Ideally all that is of value in the several religions should be taken up into this one religion; but it is possible that to begin with humanity may fall far short of this ideal, and in this way much of value may be lost. The new problem for Islamic theologians, as for those of all the religions (including Christianity) is to present what they see of value in their religion in such a form that it is capable of being assimilated by others. The present survey has been written from the standpoint that there is much of value in Islam; and it would be thus a loss for the whole world if what is valuable is not transmuted and sublimated, and so made suitable for inclusion in the unified religion for the whole world.[31]

A remarkably similar view was expressed by Radhakrishnan in his book, *The Hindu View of Life*, first published in 1927:

> The different religions are slowly learning to hold out hands of friendship to each other in every part of the world. The parliaments of religions and conferences and congresses of liberal thinkers of all creeds promote mutual understanding and harmony. The study of comparative religion is developing a fairer attitude to other religions. It is impressing on us the fundamental unity of all religions by pointing out that the genius of the people, the spirit of the age and the need of the hour determine the emphasis in each religion. We are learning to think clearly about the interrelations of religions. We tend to look upon different religions not as incompatibles but as complementaries, and so indispensable to each other for the realisation of the common end. Closer contact with other religions has dispelled the belief that only this or that religion has produced men of courage and patience, self-denying love and creative energy. Every great religion has cured its followers of the swell of passion, the thrust of desire and the blindness of temper. The crudest religion seems to have its place in the cosmic scheme, for gorgeous flowers justify the muddy roots from which they spring.[31]

The above passages express the ideal of the comparative religion movement, namely, that an examination of all the religions will lead quite naturally to a unified world religion. They show that this movement was not just confined to Christianity and that it was widespread at least until the 1960s. The comparative religion movement began in the 1870s with the attempts of scholars such as Max Müller[32] and C.P. Tiele[33] to establish a 'science of religion'. It was not strictly a response to Darwin's *Origin of*

Species, published in 1859; it was more like a response to the increasing knowledge of and interest in religions throughout the world.

The movement gathered apace during the 20th century, and perhaps its most popular exposition was in the Rev. A.C. Bouquet's book, *Comparative Religion*, published in 1941.[34] Although Bouquet was a prominent Anglican clergyman and academic, his book contains a remarkably dispassionate account of all the religions including Christianity. His avowed aim was to pinpoint the common features of all the various religions as a prelude to unifying religion in general. This is an eclectic view which gathers together all the religions without supplying a conceptual system to which they can all be referred.

The comparative religion movement was ultimately unsuccessful because its aims were too diffuse and it lacked a unified system of thought. Due to this lack of intellectual rigour, the movement petered out during the 1960s. This was not just because of the fashionable decline of religion. It was partly because the traditional religions have gradually reasserted themselves with the partial decline of the hegemony of science. The religions have rediscovered themselves as Wittgensteinian 'forms of life'.[35] They now see themselves as being independent and self-subsistent contributions to human culture, and instead of unifying themselves in the common interest of humanity, they are now engaged in a post-modern dialogue of mutual incomprehension.

While religious leaders indulge in a high-minded deference to each other's beliefs, serious-minded fundamentalists of all faiths find more direct means of enforcing their beliefs on others. This can only lead to a tribalisation of human belief systems in place of the unifying ideals of the comparative religion movement. Such divisiveness goes against the view that we should overcome our racial and national divisions to emphasize what we have in common rather than what divides us. The potential for conflict and war between competing religious blocs will remain while fundamentalists continue to preach the absolute truth of their respective religions compared with other religions whose adherents are equally convinced of the absolute truth of theirs.

The Failure of the Comparative Religion Movement

The comparative religion movement failed because it catalogued and classified religions rather than forming something new which goes beyond all religions. It was an *eclectic* enterprise which studied all religions without discriminating between them. Such eclecticism provides no conceptual system by which the various religions can be compared and contrasted. In the end, it merely shows (1) how distinctive each religion is and (2) how difficult it is to reconcile them all into one unified religion. They simply continue on their individual paths without hope or desire of converging or reconciling them.

At the other extreme, the *syncretist* approach combines one or more religions in an attempt to incorporate them. In effect a new religion results, as in the case of Sikhism which combines elements of Islam and Hinduism. Sikhism was not successful in replacing its constituent religions, any more than Islam has successfully replaced Judaism or Christianity. The most striking example of all is the religion of Baha'i which set out as a syncretic religion that includes all other religions, as this *Encyclopaedia Britannica* article shows:

> Baha`i faith, religion founded in Iran in the mid-19th century by Mirza Hoseyn 'Ali Nuri, who is known as Baha`Ullah (Arabic: "Glory of God"). The cornerstone of Baha`i belief is the conviction that Baha`Ullah and his forerunner, who was known as the Bab, were manifestations of God, who in his essence is unknowable. The principal Baha`i tenets are the essential unity of all religions and the unity of humanity. Baha`ists believe that all the founders of the world's great religions have been manifestations of God and agents of a progressive divine plan for the education of the human race. Despite their apparent differences, the world's great religions, according to the Baha`ist, teach an identical truth. Baha` Ullah's peculiar function was to overcome the disunity of religions and establish a universal faith. Baha`ists believe in the oneness of humanity and devote themselves to the abolition of racial, class, and religious prejudices. The great bulk of Baha`i teachings is concerned with social ethics; the faith has no priesthood and does not observe ritual forms in its worship.[36]

As most people today have never heard of the Baha'i faith, we can confidently say that it has failed thus far in its mission to unify all religions. Indeed, the more a religion strives to unify all religions by bettering them in some way, the more it is certain to fail because it becomes just another religion self-confidently proselytising itself as a religion. It merely adds to the sum-total of religious faiths. This includes Richard Dawkins' ill-advised attempt to replace religion with a dogmatically biological view of things in the book, *The God Delusion*. The key is to rise above all religions and incorporate them comfortably in a Vivodoxian manner without challenging their various tenets and doctrines.

Neither eclecticism nor syncretism can solve the problem of getting beyond all religions whatsoever to provide something recognisably better. *Vivodoxia* solves the problem by encompassing all religious beliefs without superseding them. It offers a philosophical standpoint within which all religious beliefs may be understood in their own rights but not without criticism. Religious extremism cannot occur when people learn to hold their beliefs at arm's length instead of regarding them as the absolute, unanswerable truth. Above all, Vivodoxia symbolises our togetherness as a species. The ways in which it can do this are considered in Part Two above.

The *Prime Principle of Life-Belief* consists in believing in life as a product of universal processes as described by science. Perhaps if religious faith can encompass this Principle then it is the key to reconciling religion to science since it makes the latter pre-eminent.

Religious leaders need a perspective that takes them above and beyond that of their respective religions. If that perspective is confined entirely to their own religion to the exclusion of every other religion or way of thinking then their preachings will be over-focused on the importance of their creed as compared with others. Their exhortations will become extreme and provocative. They will tell their followers that only their religion is true and valid and that every other way of thinking is mistaken and dangerous to their faith. This is why an overall view of religions is required to put them all in their proper place relative to our common humanity. Unless they are contributing in a positive way to humanity, they are potentially inhuman organisations. Vivodoxia or life-belief is a positive way of doing so.

The lotus flower is symbolic of life. In Hinduism, the lotus symbolises what is divine or immortal in humanity, In Buddhism, it represents the purity of mind, body, and speech. In other cultures, it is a symbol of rebirth; we suffer many ordeals in life before we blossom forth to be ourselves.

Part Six

Practical Application
in the Community

What we can do in practice

There is no need to wean people away from their own particular religions. As we have seen, there is a place for all religions in this belief system. Life-belief or *Vivodoxia* aims to bring religions together and not alienate them, least of all from each other. This can be achieved by emphasising belief in life and humanity within the ethos of community as well as the ethos of humanity as a whole. This makes the life-belief view compatible with any religion whatsoever. We all have this view in common when we do things together to celebrate the achievements and aspirations of our communities, organisations and ultimately humanity as a whole. By offering additional viewpoints that strengthen the belief in life, this strengthens the communality of all religions by showing what they all have in common.

Respect for other religions can be shown by participating in them with the aim of making them more community oriented. Life-believers can attend rites and services and emphasise their community aspects. In this way, places of worship such as churches, chapels, cathedrals, synagogues, temples and mosques can be encouraged to be more community related. They can function as community centres with their own distinct identity. They need not be exclusive places, forbidden to all but true believers. With goodwill and self-confidence in their own value to the community, they can be open to allcomers. Religious scriptures, such as the Bible, the Koran and the Bhavaga Gita, can be studied and respected for the positive contributions they make to the human condition. They can be referred to and actively discussed in relation to each other.

Anti-Exclusionarianism. The philosophy of life-belief gives every religion the opportunity to become inclusive and open to all comers. When the meeting places of all religions are treated as community centres open to all, they become inclusive of all faiths and all beliefs systems which can be discussed and not be centred on one faith to the exclusion of all the others. This anti-exclusionarianism (to coin an ugly word) can become the dominant view in society when life-belief is given a prominent position in our culture. After all, religious sects can take exclusiveness to harmful extremes which lead to such tragedies as the Jonesville massacre and the Waco disaster. They are not so much anti-social as being harmful to their own adherents by blighting and narrowing their life opportunities.

Disputation rather than sermonising. Ideally, community centres can be *disputariums* that discuss all the important questions about life and nature without answering any of them with total certitude. All the ministers, priests, rabbis, mullahs, ayatollahs and preachers in general can become qualified *disputants* who interact with their respective assemblages as equals in a sincere quest for truth and understanding. We can still have moving ceremonies, rites and rituals, but let them be seen as life-enhancing rites of passage or as historical pageants and not just the exclusive and mystical reserve of particular religions.

Community centres can embody the ethos of the community in a practical and non-mystical way. Local traditions might be used, similar to the celebrated Groundhog Day in Punxsutawney, Pennsylvania[37] to help us to unite the present with the past without commitment to religious doctrines of any kind. An even more outstanding example of a community unified by a local tradition is the annual Up-Helly-Aa fire festival in Lerwick in the Shetland Isles.[38] This tradition is largely a late 19th century invention based loosely on the Norse traditions of the islands. Significantly, it has become an isolated tradition rather than a revival of pagan Norse religion. It has proved to be hugely popular and an effective tourist attraction.

Such traditions unify the whole community and give it an identity and common purpose. Religious centres fulfilled such a role in medieval times when their dominance was absolute. But nowadays they alienate people with their inhuman ideals and unattainable divine aspirations. The absoluteness of their beliefs pitches the various religions and sects against each other. Thus, the vivodoxian aspiration towards unity is required nowadays because of the very divisiveness of religion. This is especially so when true believers take up arms in the name of their respective beliefs. Their strong beliefs may give meaning to their empty lives but lead to needless conflicts with those with equally strong and incompatible beliefs. Unless they emphasise what they have in common more than their differences, such sectarian conflict seems inevitable. Vivodoxia has the merit of emphasising what they all have in common.

The community centres advocated here can be self-financing charities within their respective communities. They should be free to organise themselves to serve their communities appropriately. Each centre can find its own way to represent what is best and worthwhile in the ethos of its community. No two centres would be the same in the lectures, courses, discussions, ceremonies, recreations or whatever activities that they consider appropriate, rewarding and uplifting to offer their respective communities. Thus, there is no need for overbearing hierarchies or authorities stultifying their good works.

Perhaps there would also be an opportunity for wealthy individuals who are prepared to support such centres. They might be encouraged to do so by having centres named after them. This could be their bid for immortality and it would also encourage them to get involved with their respective communities, just as soccer club owners engage with their clubs. This is not an unusual proposal as all kinds of charitable organisations adopt the names of individuals: schools, hospitals and universities and their buildings are often named after wealthy benefactors.

However, there is no need for these centres to be named after people already well known to the public. The limit can be drawn on stars, celebrities, politicians and others already well known to the public.

The Ethos of the Community

An ethos is the spirit of a united community. A unified and purposeful community, whether in the form of a neighbourhood, village or district, has an ethos distinct to itself when its inhabitants identify strongly with it. They have interests and activities in common which bring them together and make the community more meaningful to them than it is otherwise. The ethos is manifested when they come together physically in meetings and when they recognise what they have in common as a community. Their inner will as individuals is both raised and augmented as a result. They become more developed and self-possessed persons because of their belonging to something that involves them as unique personalities.

This aspect of the ethos is important because our constant involvement in a community of our fellow human beings provides external limitations to the ethos. Contributing to the community disciplines our inner development and ensures that it grows and develops meaningfully and purposefully. Constantly interacting with other persons challenges us and makes us more aware of our ingrained uniqueness. In partaking of the ethos of the community we find a sense of belonging that is essential to our well-being and personal development.

These centres can rally the community by appealing to tradition and history rather than religion and authority. Religion is admissible in forming part of that tradition and provides valuable insight into the human condition. It is no longer admissible as a body of ultimate or absolute truth commanding obedience and submission. It is a body of learning and instruction that benefits of each individual on a personal level rather than a means of inducing their obedience and subservience.

The Ethos of Humanity

We participate in the ethos of humanity whenever we empathise with our fellow human beings when they are afflicted by pandemics, famines, earthquakes, tsunamis, terrorist attacks and so on. It is an additional dimension of ourselves and an expression of our human feelings. It is not the same as the idea of humanity which has been misused by utopian ideologists to justify killing and torturing their fellow human beings. In that case, the idea has become more important than people and is treated in an absolutist way. In contrast, the ethos of humanity is not above and beyond us but an intimate part of what we are as individuals. It is more concerned with our sympathetic feelings about other people than with what we think of them in any critical or hostile way.

The ethos of humanity is particularly important in uniting us as a species against the racial, national, religious, sectarian or economic divisions that forever threaten to turn us against each other in self-destructive war and conflict. The slogan, *Amate l'Umanità!*, (love humanity!) was used by the great Italian patriot, Giuseppe Mazzini (1805-1872), in his campaign to unify the disparate nations and city states of Italy.[39] He argued that the interests of humanity are more important than those of family and country. The creation of a united Italy was more vital to humanity than loyalty to smaller units which were perpetually in conflict with each other.

Another example is the 18th century Scottish Enlightenment. Its whole ethos consisted in a regard for humanity which arose when the identity of the Scottish nation was subsumed into that of Great Britain with the union of parliaments in 1707. That regard for humanity made sense of the loss of Scottish political identity. The Scots saw that their higher duty lay in serving humanity with their literary, scientific, architectural and other efforts, and that this was worth sacrificing national identity. The same applies to religion in general. The duty of every religion is to see itself in the context of humanity, otherwise it sets itself all too easily above the rest of humanity and therefore against it, as has been argued throughout this book. But religion is not the only threat to humanity, the assertion of nation states against other nation states is an even greater threat.

Life-belief helps us to blend our patriotism into the communality of humanity. Every human culture has its place in our common humanity just as every religion has its place therein. The job and joy of life-belief is to bring them all together in one happy family, hopefully. In the homely Scottish saying, "Wir a' Jock Tamson's bairns"[40] which means "We are all like the children belonging to the same human family". Life-belief offers company and fellowship to all those desiring it. It aims to bring people together with the common ends of benefiting each other and society as a whole. The human race is treated as an enlarged family that embraces everyone. No one is excluded from the family of humanity because we are all the same in being human beings. Thus, there is only one admissible form of racism – human racism, since there is only one race, the human race.

The mission of this faith is therefore to stress our communality. What we have in common is far more important than what divides us into disparate nations, cultures and languages. Our love of life embraces a love of humanity as the best means by which life can be prolonged and fostered on this planet. But human beings lose the bigger picture too easily in favour of ephemeral passions such as those of religious fervour, nationalism, or ideological fanaticism of whatever kind. The lure of charismatically inspired crazes can surely be countered by the cool and sturdy reason of life-belief. Life is what we make of it as individuals, and it is not necessary to submit entirely to the dictations of long dead writers and thinkers to satisfy self-serving religious hierarchies.

The Last Word

"Not God but life, more life, a larger, richer, more satisfying life, is in last analysis the end of religion. The love of life at any and every level of development, or, to use another phraseology, the instinct for preservation and increase, is the religious impulse. It would appear, then, that there is at bottom no specifically "religious" impulse; the preservation and increase of life is the moving impulse as well of religious as of secular activity."

James H. Leuba[41]

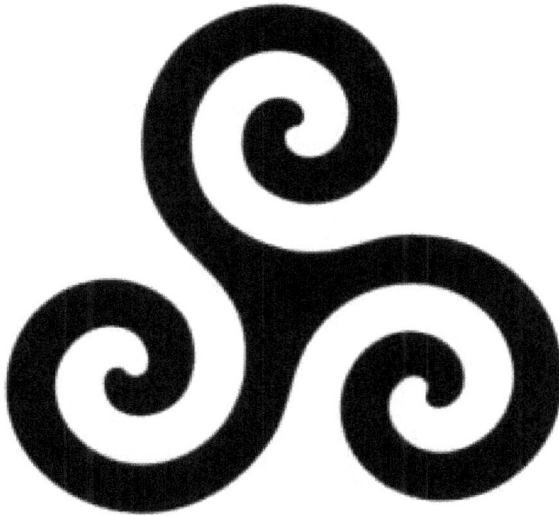

This triskele symbol consists of three interconnected spirals linking infinity with life and fertility. It is found in Neolithic and Celtic cultures, as well as in later classical times. The Greek word τρισκελής (*triskelés*) means 'three-legged', and the symbol is often represented as three linked legs. Also, three times three is the length of pregnancy.

Notes and References

1. Alfred Tennyson (1809-1892), *In Memoriam*, Canto 56. Available online: http://www.online-literature.com/tennyson/718/

2. Cf. the following website: https://www.sciencealert.com/meta-analysis-finds-majority-of-human-pregnancies-end-in-miscarriage-biorxiv

3. Jonathan Swift (1667-1745), "Thoughts on Various Subjects", *Minor Satires*, 1706.

4. Natiionalism means war. « Le nationalisme c'est la guerre! » as François Mitterrand said in a speech to the European Parliament on 17th January 1995.

5. Adapted from the diagram in "The Correlation of Structure, Action and Thought", by T. Lauder Brunton (1844-1916) in *The Popular Science Monthly*, ed. by William Jay Youmans, Vol. XLII, Nov. 1892 to Apr. 1893, New York: D. Appleton & Co., 1883, p. 752. This diagram comes from an unstated work by Ernst Haeckel (1834-1919). See Haeckel's Wikipedia biography for more detailed diagrams showing how these species develop differently as embryos.

6. From *The Code of Hammurabi*, available in this Yale Law School, Avalon Project website: https://avalon.law.yale.edu/ancient/hamframe.asp

7. Cf. Friedrich Nietzsche (1844-1900), *Human, All too Human* (1878). London: Penguin, 1994, p. 170.

8. The metaphor of the 'invisible hand' was used by Adam Smith (1723-1790) in both his main works:

(1) In the *Moral Sentiments*, it is rich people who "are led by an invisible hand . . without intending it, without knowing it, advance the interest of society", *The Theory of Moral Sentiments*, (1759). London: H.G. Bohn, 1853, Part IV, Ch. I, p. 265.

(2) In *The Wealth of Nations*, it is the worker or businessman who is "led by an invisible hand to promote an end which was no part of his intention. By pursuing his own interest, he frequently promotes that of the society more effectually than when he really intends to promote it." *An Inquiry into the Nature and Causes of the Wealth of Nations*, (1776). London: Routledge, 1900, Book IV, Ch. II, p. 345.

9. Adam Smith, *The Theory of Moral Sentiments* (1759), London: H.G. Bohn, 1853, Part III, ch I, para. 2, p. 161f.

10. Francis Hutcheson (1694-1746), *An Inquiry into the Original of our Ideas of Beauty, and Virtue, in Two Treatises.* 4th Edition, Corrected. (1738), Treatise II, *An Inquiry Concerning Moral Good and Evil,* Section III, §7, p. 177f. The same passages are also available in *Philosophical Works,* ed. By R.S. Downie. London: J.M. Dent, 1994, pp. 79, 88 etc.

11. Immanuel Kant (1724-1804), *The Moral Law,* (*Groundwork of the*

Metaphysics of Morals, 1785), trans. H.J. Paton, London: Hutchinson, 1972, pp. 60-62.

12. The full etymology of 'prospective' is as follows: Middle English *prospectyve*, n., from Old French *prospectif*, an adjective (as a noun, *prospective*, feminine) = Italian *prospettivo*, from Late Latin *prospectivus*, pertaining to a prospect or to looking forward, from Latin *prospicere*, past participle *prospectus*, look forward, look into the distance.

13. H.G. Wells, (1866-1946), *The Discovery of the Future* (1902), ed. by P. Parrinder, London: PNL Press, 1989, p. 19.

14. H.G. Wells (1902), *op. cit.*, p. 20.

15. Cf. My paper, 'World War One and the Loss of the Humanist Consensus' which is reproduced in my book, *American Papers on Humanism and Religion*, (Almostic Publications, 2014), pp.72-94.

16. Auguste Comte (1798–1857), Comte's absurd form of religion was taken up in Victorian England where four temples of humanity - two in London, one each in Liverpool and Newcastle - were established. The Liverpool temple lingered on till 1947 when it was sold and became the Third Church of Christ Scientist. Its statue of humanity (a mother with child) appropriately 'gathered dust in Liverpool Maternity Hospital'. Cf. Terence R. Wright, *The Religion of Humanity: The Impact of Comtean Positivism on Victorian Britain*, Cambridge: CUP, 1986, p. 260.

17. H.G. Wells (1902), *op. cit.,* p. 36.

18. For example, Bill Gates, Elon Musk and the late Stephen Hawking have intimated in newspaper interviews their concerns about artificial intelligence being more of a threat than a benefit to our future (though in recent years their views may have changed). Cf. Katya Siepmann and Annabella McIntosh, 'The Age of Transhumanism Has Begun: Will It Bring Humanism to Its End? – An Interview with Roland Benedikter.' *Essays in the Philosophy of Humanism*, Sheffield: Equinox Publishing Ltd., 2015, Vol. 23.2, p. 136.

19. As listed in Siepmann and McIntosh, *op. cit.* p. 142.

20. Isaac Asimov (1920–1992), 'Runaround', *I, Robot,* New York: Doubleday & Company, 1950.

21. Pierre Teilhard de Chardin, (1881-1955), *The Phenomenon of Man* (1955). London: Collins, 1965, p. 283f.

22. The phrase 'global village' was first coined by Marshall McLuhan (1911-1980) in *The Gutenberg Galaxy: The Making of Typographic* Man, Toronto: University of Toronto Press, 1962, p. 31.

23. Pierre Teilhard de Chardin, *Activation of Energy,* trans. René Hague. New York and London: Harcourt Brace Jovanovich, 1970, p. 284.

24. Excerpted from the article in the following *Encyclopaedia Britannica* website: https://www.britannica.com/biography/Pierre-Teilhard-de-Chardin

25. William James (1842-1910), *The Varieties of Religious Experience*,

1902. London: Fontana, 1960, Lecture XX, p. 468.

26. Bertrand Russell (1872-1970), *Why I am not a Christian,* 'Has Religion Made Useful Contributions to Religion? 1957, London: Unwin Paperbacks, 1989, ch.2, p. 42.

27. William James, *op. cit.*, p. 487.

28. Samuel Johnson (1709-1784), *The Rambler*, no. 60, Sat. 13th Oct. 1750, in *Selected Writings of Samuel* Johnson, ed. by Patrick Cruttwell. London: Penguin Books, 1986, Part II, p.169.

29. A.C. Bouquet (1884–1976), *The Sacred Books of the World.* London: Penguin, 1954.

30. W. M. Watt (1909-2006), *Islamic Philosophy and Theology,* Edinburgh University Press, 1962, p.178.

31. Sarvepalli Radhakrishnan (1888-1975), *The Hindu View of Life* (1927). London: Unwin Books, 1960, p.43.

32. Cf. Friedrich Max Müller (1823-1900), *Lectures on the Origin and Growth of Religion as Illustrated by the Religions of India* (1878).

33. Cf. Cornelis Petrus Tiele (1830-1902), *Outlines of the History of Religion: to the Spread of the Universal Religions* (1877), trans. J. E. Carpenter.

34. A.C. Bouquet (1884–1976), *Comparative Religion.* London: Penguin Books, 1941.

35. Cf. Ludwig Wittgenstein (1889-1951), *Philosophical Investigations* (1953), trans. by G.E.M. Anscombe. Oxford: Blackwell, 1968, §23, p. 11. This inimical concept of 'forms of life' differentiates human activities without showing what they have in common. It is acontextual and ignores the hierarchy of contexts in which religions and the sciences form part of the context of humanity that is higher and more important than what divides us at a local level.

36. The article is available at the following *Encyclopaedia Britannica* website: http://www.britannica.com/topic/Bahai-Faith

37. Cf. http://www.groundhog.org/about/history.php

38. Cf. http://www.shetlandtourism.com/pages/up_helly_aa.htm

39. Giuseppe Mazzini (1805–1872), *The Duties of Man*, London: J.M. Dent & Co. 1915, pp. 49-50.

40. "Wir a' Jock Tamson's bairns." This Scottish saying does not translate well into standard English – "We are all John Thomson's children". It is too literal. The Scots language differs from English in having peremptory undertones and unspoken implications. It is not known for certain who this person was but perhaps the best candidate is John Thomson (1778-1840) who was a minister of Duddingston Kirk in Edinburgh from 1805 till his death. He had two wives (not at once!) and ten children – five sons and five daughters. (Cf. Hew Scott, *Fasti Ecclesiae Scoticanae: The Succession of Ministers in the Church of Scotland from the*

Reformation, Edinburgh: Oliver & Boyd, 1915, Vol. One, p. 20).

    41. James H. Leuba (1868-1946), "The Contents of Religious Consciousness",*The Monist*, xi. 572, July, 1901. The passage is quoted by William James in *The Varieties of Religious Experience,* (London: Fontana, 1960, Conclusion, p.483). However, William James fails to see the significance of this approach as he thinks a science of religion can only come from studying the unconscious psychological foundations of religious thinking. Leuba himself does not develop any further the thoughts contained in this quotation, as his paper is concerned with the psychological aspects of religion.

The phoenix is a legendary immortal bird that regenerates cyclically. It is symbolic of how we live our lives, when we discard negative energy and rid ourselves of bad habits. We then regenerate ourselves by giving birth to more positive thinking and a healthier way of life.

Index

Akhenaton celebrates the life-giving attributes of the Sun in the first monotheistic religion which was later preached by Moses to the Israelites. Moses may have been a priest or follower of Akhenaton's religion. Freud was also of that view in his book *Moses and Monothesism* (1939).

Appendix A
Some Notable Sayings in this Book

There is nothing to beat the marvellous gift of life, and it surely deserves to be celebrated for its own sake, regardless of religious considerations. (Preface, p. vi)

There is no room for religious resignation or monkish silence in life-belief. It is about living life to the full. This is *vivoplenia* involving the principle of plenitude. (Preface, p. vi)

Believing in life is about the living of it and not the deification of it. A philosophy of *living* is intended by this book. (Introduction, p. vii)

If life-belief is universally accepted, it could bring together all religions in sharing the common faith of believing in life. Religious people can be more content with their differences from each other within the broad framework of life-belief. The religions would be less inclined to compete and vie with each other for people's attention. (Introduction, p. viii)

If we accept the view that we make our own meaning in life, then the meaning of life is the meaning we put into it, get out of it, make of it or find in it. (p.2) It can never be repeated too often that there is no meaning in the universe except what is brought into existence by living beings pursuing their ingiven purposes. (p. 3)

Life is the gift of the universe, not as creator but as facilitator. (p. 9)

The more we dread the nothingness of death, the more we value the somethingness of life. The wonderful gift of life is better appreciated when we face up to the ending of life forever when we die. (p. 14)

The need of god or any spiritual presence palls into insignificance when we are too involved in life and living to feel any need for such things belonging to the past. (p. 16)

Vivoplenia is also about life-long education. We never stop learning new facts and skills from cradle to grave. (p. 16)

We must judge our actions by the tribunal of future generations. Wars and conflicts contribute nothing of lasting value to posterity. They contribute only to the history of human folly. (p. 31)

Science tells that life is self-sustaining and needs no external influences. Each life-form develops inwardly by interacting with its environment and by building up its internal complexity over time. This internal activity is here called 'inner being'. It is an entirely physical process that is not spiritual or non-material in any way. The phrase 'inner being' is preferred over non-material words such as 'mind', 'spirit' and 'soul' which are assumed to exist as substances apart from the physical activity of the brain and body. 'Inner being' refers to the processes occurring in the brain and body that make possible our self-identity and subjectivity. These unifying processes make possible the 'I', 'self' or 'ego'. (p. 28)

The human self is discontinuous and fragmentary, and is liable to fall apart completely unless it is constantly bolstered and reinforced by positive thinking and by restrained and purposeful behaviour. To counter this desultory tendency, we must constantly strive to bring ourselves together in terms of our aims and goals in life. We achieve this by introspection to monitor our behaviour and organise ourselves in a positive and disciplined way. We thereby build up our inner life and become more integrated and purposeful in thought and behaviour. This is the aim of *vivoplenia* as outlined in part three of this book. (p. 38)

We may consider ourselves god-like in creating the universe for ourselves as we imbibe more and more information about it. But we must also humble ourselves by realising the extent of our ignorance and of our smallness in relation to the unimaginable vastness of the universe. [p. 43)

Love is the prime unifying force in the universe. This is love in the sense of things coming together to interact harmoniously. . . . . Love has no real meaning unless it contributes to unity and harmony and the future of humanity, as in the case of reproduction or creative activity of some kind. (p. 51)

The complex social structures of mammals have led to human beings, the most cultured, devious and deadly of all animals. (p. 53)

We can all be *Christians* in our attitude towards our potential enemies and in our attempts to understand people rather than hate them. Equally, we can all be *Jews* in our respect for family life; *Muslims* in our respect for authority and absolute values; Buddhists in our use of meditation to reach our inner being; *Hindus* in our appreciation of spirituality; and so on. In this way, we can make use of the strengths of truths in particular religions. (p. 58).

Appendix B
Youth [1914]*

By
Dr. Frank Crane (1861-1928)

Youth is not a time of life; it is a state of mind. It is not a matter of ripe cheeks, red lips, and supple knees; it is a temper of the will, a quality of the imagination, a vigor of the emotions. It is the freshness of the deep springs of life.

Youth means a temperamental predominance of courage over timidity, of the appetite for adventure over the love of ease. This often exists in a man of fifty more than in a boy of twenty.

Nobody grows old by merely living a number of years. People grow old only by deserting their ideals.

Years wrinkle the skin; but to give up enthusiasm wrinkles the soul.

Worry, doubt, self-disgust, fear, and despair – these are the long, long years that bow the heart and turn the greening spirit back to dust.

Whether sixty or sixteen, there is in every human being's heart the lure of wonder, the sweet amazement at the stars and at starlike things and thoughts, the undaunted challenge of events, the unfailing, childlike appetite for what next, and the joy of the game of living.

You are as young as your faith, as old as your doubt; as young as your self-confidence, as old as your fear; as young as your hope, as old as your despair.

In the central place of your heart is an evergreen tree; its name is Love. So long as it flourishes you are young. When it dies you are old.

In the central place of your heart there is a wireless station. So long as it receives messages of beauty, hope, cheer, grandeur, courage, and power from the earth, from men, and from the Infinite, so long are you young. When the wires are down, and all the central place of your heart is covered with the snows of cynicism and ice of pessimism, then you are grown old, even at twenty, and may God have mercy upon your soul!

* *Cosmopolitan*, May 1914, volume 56, number 6, p. 721. While it is not true that old age is nothing but a state of mind, it can be made more tolerable by maintaining the optimistic state of mind so brilliantly expressed in this essay. Parts of this essay have been quoted as the sayings of other people, such as General Douglas Macarthur who had a quotation from this essay hung on the wall of his office.

Appendix C
The Wisdom of Roman Virtues
Part One – A Systematic List of the Virtues
I. The Virtues of Good Character

Auctoritas
> "Spiritual Authority" The sense of one's social standing, built up through experience, Pietas, and Industria.

Constantia:
> "Constancy" Firmness of purpose and reliability.

Dignitas
> "Dignity" A sense of self-worth, personal pride.

Firmitas
> "Tenacity" Strength of mind, the ability to stick to one's purpose.

Gravitas
> "Gravity" A sense of the importance of the matter at hand, responsibility and earnestness. It is the opposite of *levitas*, a quality the Romans despised as it means trifling when you should be serious.

Honestas
> "Respectability" The honour and respect received from others through having a reputation for good character, integrity, uprightness, and probity. The image that one presents as a respectable member of society.

Humanitas
> "Humanity" Refinement, civilization, learning, and being cultured.

Industria
> "Industriousness" Hard work and application.

Liberalitas
> "Liberality" Generous giving.

Nobilitas
> "Nobility" Noble action within the public sphere.

Patientia
> "Endurance, Patience" The ability to weather storms and crisis.

Prudentia
> "Prudence" Foresight, wisdom, and personal discretion.

Severitas
> "Sternness" Self-control. Being severe with one's self.

Veritas
> "Truthfulness" Sincerity and trustworthiness in dealing with others.

II. The Virtues of Wholesomeness (Integrity)

Frugalitas

> "Frugalness" Economy and simplicity of style, without being miserly.

Pudicita

> "Modesty, Chastity." A public expression which belies the accusation of "moral corruptness" in ancient Rome.

Salubritas

> "Wholesomeness" Health and cleanliness.

Simplicitas

> "The simple life" The quality of the man who sees things clearly and sees them as they are - that is, keeping one's feet planted firmly on the ground

Virtus

> "Manliness" The vitality and energy associated with virile assertion. "Courage" Especially of leaders within society and government.

III. The Virtues of Good Humour

Comitas

> "Humour" Ease of manner, courtesy, openness, and friendliness.

Hilaritas

> "Mirth, rejoicing" An expression of happy times.

Laetitia

> "Joy, Gladness" The celebration of thanksgiving, often of the resolution of crisis.

IV. The Virtues of Mercy and Justice

Aequitas

> "Equity" Fair dealing both within government and among the people.

Clementia

> "Mercy" Mildness and gentleness.

Concordia

> "Concord" Harmony among the Roman people, and also between Rome and other nations.

Iustitia

> "Justice" As expressed by sensible laws and governance.

Pietas

> "Dutifulness" More than religious piety; a respect for the natural order socially, politically, and religiously. It includes ideas of patriotism and devotion to others.

V. The Virtues of Social Order

Abundantia

"Abundance, Plenty" The ideal of there being enough food and prosperity for all segments of society.

Felicitas

"Happiness, prosperity" A celebration of the best aspects of Roman society.

Fides

"Confidence" Trust, dependability and good faith in all commercial and governmental dealings.

Fortuna

"Fortune" An acknowledgement of positive events.

Genius

"Spirit of Rome" Acknowledgement of the combined spirit of Rome, and its people.

Libertas

"Freedom" This virtue has been subsequently aspired to by all cultures.

Ops

"Wealth" Acknowledgement of the prosperity of the Roman world. The importance of wealth generation to a developing society.

Pax

"Peace" A celebration of peace among society and between nations.

Providentia

"Providence, Forethought" The ability of Roman society to survive trials and manifest a greater destiny.

Salus

"Safety" Concern for public health and welfare.

Securitas

"Confidence, Security" Brought by peace and efficient governance.

Spes

"Hope" Especially during times of difficulty.

Uberitas

"Fertility" Particularly concerning agriculture.

Part Two – Applying These Virtues

Taking them to extremes. The problem with all these virtues is that they can be taken to extremes and lose their value in the process. Their uncritical application by Roman rulers contributed to the ultimate downfall of the Roman Republic. For example, authority (*auctoritas*) became outright tyranny in the hands of the Roman Emperors. It is therefore necessary to distinguish the positive and negative usages of these virtues since they easily become vices when taken to extremes.

I. Good Character

Positive Usage. The wise person's good character is enhanced greatly by the virtue of gravity (*gravitas*) when it is accompanied by dignity, severity and firmness (*dignitas*, *severitas*, and *firmitas*). The resolution and purposefulness of such a person is not to be doubted. It gives them authority *auctoritas*) because people look up to them as having nobility and liberality (*nobilitas*) and (*liberalitas*).

The Romans emphasised humanity (*humanitas*) in the sense of learning and depth of thought. Without these, a man cannot become a scholar and a gentleman. We also need constancy (*constantia*) in being reliable people. Patience (*patentia*) enables us to put up with inconveniences in expectation of better things in the future. Only with industriousness (*industria*) can we be useful citizens contributing value and profit to the community. Without foresight and wisdom (*prudential*) many a person's life is ruined by excessive self-indulence and self-abuse, both physical and mental.

Negative Usage. The 'virtue' of authority (*auctoritas*) was easily taken to extremes as those with it could be used by those in authority to commit violence and murder with impunity. Thus, the *auctoritas* even of Vestal Virgins gave them the right to beat and execute people. This was symbolised by the *fasces* - the bundle of axe and sticks used for that purpose. If there is too much severity and gravity, then callousness and inhumanity creeps in. Humanity in the sense of respecting the lives and liberties of individuals only came with Christianity.

II. Wholesomeness and Integrity

Positive Usage. Wholesomeness (*salubritas*) consists in seeing things as a whole. Restraint is achieved by frugality and modesty (*frugalitas* and *pudicita*) which leads to simplicity (*simplicitas*) – the simple life – and to virtue (*virtus*) without which is required for great and resounding deeds.

Negative Usage.
Too much of these virtues alienates the élite from the masses. They get above themselves and forget that they are mortal like the rest of us – *memento mori* – 'remember you must die' – as the victorious were told as they rode in their triumphal chariots. An overemphasis on the simple life, leads to the comforts of civilised life being removed. One is reminded by the fate of the great movie mogul, Howard Hughes who finished up a naked ascetic repudiating all human comforts altogether in search of simplest possible way of living.

III. Good Humour
Positive Usage. We all need joy (*laetitia*), mirth (*hilaritas*) and humour (*comitas*) in our lives. *Laetitia* in particular reflects the joy of living. It helps us to overcome all the grief and grievances that life can throw at us. *Hilaritas* (mirth) and *comitas* (humour) is required to relieve us from the pain of daily living.

Negative Usage. We can always have too much of a good thing and this applies also to good humour. Mirth and humour can be a distraction from facing realities and getting things done that need to be done. The laughter of crowds at the gladiatorial games would be reflect their bloodthirstiness when they thought it funny to see people begging for their lives.

IV. Mercy and Justice
Positive Usage. Showing mercy (*clementia*) is part of being human. It leads us to behave with justice (*iustitia*) and equity (*aequitia*) in our dealings with each other. Out of dutifulness (*pietas*), we respect society and take our peaceful place in it, thus ensuring concord (*concordia*).
Negative Usage. Negativity arises when these virtues are applied legalistically. When the law is imposed without any bounds, the citizen is enslaved by it. Laws can become more important than the people on whom they are foisted. They were the tools of authority to impose its will on people and therefore they reflected the will of the emperors in the end.

V. Social Order
Positive Usage. The spirit (*genius*) of the Roman people depended on their adherence to the community spirit which underlies good fortuna (fortune). The *libertas* and *felicitas* (liberty and happiness) of the people lies at the foundation of social order. Unless their liberty is maintained and sustained, the people will decreasingly submit to the social order. But their happiness is for nought without the means to live well, and there is no freedom to do as one pleases. Hence the need for sufficient wealth (*Ops*)

in society to ensure *abundantia* (plenty). Without this, there is no largesse to be distributed, no capital for business purposes, and no funds for public events and performances. The *pax* (peace), *securitas* (security) and *salus* (safety) of the people is threatened. The future *providentia* (welfare) and *fides* (confidence) of the people depends on all these things and there is no *spes* (hope) left.

Negative Usage. The liberty of the people was the least of the concerns of later Roman Emperors. They were concerned only with their freedom to do as they please. The whole *genius* (spirit) of the people was suborned to the will of the Emperor. The liberty and happiness of the latter became more important than that of individuals. The Roman Emperors used their wealth to appease the people with bread and circuses. Peace was purchased at the price of reducing their enemies to penury and slavery.

Conclusion: This elaboration of the Roman Virtues brings them up to date by considering both their positive and negative sides. This hopefully makes them more relevant to the complexities of the modern world which is presently beset with negative events around us. The Roman Empire failed because of the predominance of negative attitudes, such as its inability to look to the future and its failure to value life above all else. The ultimate aim of Life-Belief or Vivodoxia is of course the promotion of life and the importance of valuing it everywhere. This combats the negativity involved in applying the Roman Virtues, a negativity which still emerges in the religions of today when their beliefs are applied to unreasonable extremes. Unless we stand up for ourselves in a positive way, we might as well give way to a more advanced 'species' of self-generating AI machines.